DIARY OF A
SALES MANAGER

Michael Beer

MERCURY

First published in 1991
by Mercury Books
Gold Arrow Publications Limited, 862 Garratt Lane, London SW17 0NB

Set in Plantin by Phoenix Photosetting, Chatham, Kent
Printed and bound in Great Britain by Mackays of Chatham, PLC, Chatham, Kent

British Library Cataloguing in Publication Data
Beer, Michael *1926–*
   The diary of a sales manager.
   1. Sales, management
   I. Title
   658.81

   ISBN 1–85252–048–5

How it started

When Annabel gave me this book as one of my Christmas presents she said, 'You are always making notes on the backs of cigarette packets, old shopping lists and my knitting patterns. Now you have a *real* note book.'

Of course, it's much too big to be a note book: too big and too good. It's bound in what could be leather except that these days you can't tell, and the pages are heavy paper in that off-white colour which looks expensive.

Anyway, it's too grand for the sort of notes I make. No way am I going to scribble in this volume things like: 'Get DB to check slow-movings' or 'Assoc. dinner – black tie?' or even: 'Smoked 33 yesterday – cut down!'

So, I'll do what I have been promising myself I'll do for ages; I'll keep a diary. Not the sort of diary which Dorcas keeps for me which is a cross between an appointments book and a tickler file. This one will be much more detailed and – vital point – will be for my eyes only. A diary is useless unless you put everything into it, and that includes your most secret thoughts, ideas and actions. Which means that nobody else in this wide world sees it – not Annabel my ever-loving, not D-M my MD – nobody. On these beautiful pages I shall put down my triumphs and disasters, successes and failures, good deeds and bad deeds.

I'll do it for a year and see how it works out. By that time I'll probably be heartily sick of it and I'll burn the thing, but let's try it for this year at least. Today is New Year's Eve and tomorrow seems a good time to start.

It's all true, you know. I have changed names and details but, as every working Sales Manager can testify, this is what happens.

Also by Michael Beer and published by Mercury Books:

The Joy of Selling
The Joy of Winning
Break the Rules in Selling
Lead to Succeed

January

1 Monday

Well, I hope my recording angel was wide awake today and putting down everything on the right side. Since it was the last day of my leave I had a brilliant idea and took Pete and Angie off Annabel's hands for most of the day and let her do house-person things or even put her feet up and watch daytime soaps, except that she would never do that. It was cold, but bright and clear, and we went for a long walk in the forest, coming back through the village and having lunch at the Wimpy. Astonishing how Angie at the age of five and weighing about as much as two flat bricks can put away two burgers, a pile of chips the size of a slagheap and a double-thick milkshake, while Pete, already solid as a rock at the age of eight and a bit, eats half a hot dog and some coleslaw while lecturing his sister on the evils of excess carbohydrate and fried food.

Back home in the afternoon I helped Pete to put his Christmas present Lego together. It is an enormous space station, very complicated, and I suppose that if I hadn't helped him he would have had it done in half the time. Then I read to Angie out of some of her Christmas present books while she got Barbie ready for her marriage to Ken. (I hadn't realised that they had been living in sin all this time.)

It's evening and I am going through my briefcase preparing for my first day back at work tomorrow. On the floor at my feet Pete is doing exactly the same thing with his school case. I catch his eye and we sigh; no words needed.

Annabel gives me a specially warm kiss before she goes off for her bath. This could be thanks for spending time with the children (and damn it, I don't do it enough), it could be a sample of delights to come later, or it could simply be that she has realised that from tomorrow I shall no longer be under her feet all day long. I hope for

1

the second alternative, but I'm prepared to assume the last.

I have enjoyed the break but I can't wait to get back into harness. Like an old warhorse, creaky-jointed, spavined, sway-backed and scarred, the sound of the bugles, as it were, makes me totter to my feet, snort and paw the ground. Good thing, too; when I don't look forward to getting back into battle it will be time to find another line of work.

January

2 Tuesday

First day back, and easier than it could have been. A welcoming kiss from Dorcas who seems truly glad to see me. D-M looks in for a moment and hopes that I had a good holiday, 'because this year is going to be a busy one' – as if last year was a doddle. D-M is Harold Dunsby-Martin, Managing Director of Hutton Horner PLC, and my superior.

Except that once when I used that term to Annabel she shook her head. 'No. He may be your Managing Director but nowhere is it written that he is your superior.' I tried to explain that it was the usual way of putting it but she put on that 'I'm not listening to you' look of hers. 'If he is your superior then you are his inferior, and I don't accept that.'

Well, neither do I, come to that.

Anyway, I report to Harold Dunsby-Martin and to a large extent my destiny in Hutton Horner PLC is in his hands, calloused and scarred as they are from doing things with ropes (or do they call them sheets?) in his twelve-metre racing yacht.

Dorcas presented me with a pile of papers, representing work, which had accumulated while I was away. It didn't look as formidable as I had feared, and a lot of it was yellow flimsies, which meant copies of letters already written.

I said, 'Is this it? Nothing more?'

Dorcas said, 'There was plenty more. Mr Bird and I handled it among us.'

'Between us.'

'Between us. Thank you.'

Dorcas is fifty-two-years-old and an inch under five foot, and I could pick her up with one hand and throw her across the room. She is Hungarian and is the *Mittel-Europa* version of a countess. She speaks five languages fluently, but is still working on English. Her name is completely unpronounceable and everyone calls her Mrs W. Except for me. Once, when she had done something extraordinary, I congratulated her and she said complacently, 'Oh, I am full of good works.' So, like the lady in the Bible, she became Dorcas to me.

I inherited Dorcas from my predecessor and when I first came up against her unorthodox treatment of the English language, I wondered what my letters were going to look like. 'Don't worry,' Bert Corley had said. 'She's an absolute gem.' She has turned out to be more than a gem; she is now indispensable.

I began going through the pile of paper. A lot of it was routine and Dorcas and Dicky Bird had indeed handled it. Dicky is my Sales Correspondent, a sort of assistant to the Sales Manager, who does most of the admin. work for the Sales Division and acts as a contact man and clearing house for the salesmen when they phone the office, as they do once a day – or if they don't, they had better have a broken leg as a reason for not phoning. This is one of the cast-iron rules which I laid down when I took over this job: I want to know that each one of my people has been in contact with the office, no matter how briefly, every working day of their lives. Apart from the obvious reason that we may have something urgent to tell them, I want them to feel that they are not out there on their own, that they still belong to us.

I was sorting the pile of paper into smaller piles – filing, action this day, action this week – when I came upon an unopened envelope addressed to me with CONFIDENTIAL and TO BE OPENED ONLY BY ADDRESSEE written all over it in red. I said, 'All right, Dorcas, thank you. You and Dicky seem to have done a great job.'

She said, 'It was nothing. You could have stayed away twice as long and still no problems.'

I said, 'Thanks very much indeed,' to her departing back.

I slit open the envelope. I had been waiting impatiently for it. We need two more sales people and for the first time we have used a recruiting agency. Not to do the preliminary interviews but to do a vetting job on the shortlist and to give us reports on the people we had picked. These were the reports.

First report was on Henry Snape. Henry had been one of my favourites. He had come across as a real *people* person, likeable, straightforward, and he sounded as keen as mustard to get cracking in the selling business. No sales experience (he was a physical training instructor in the Navy) but that has never bothered me; if they have the right attitude, I'll make something of them.

I paged through Henry's report. There was a fair amount of four-syllable words describing the reactions to and the achievements in the various tests; most specialist organisations, no matter what field they may be in, feel that it is necessary to include a sprinkling of pretentious bullshit in their reports – it makes it look as if they have earned their outrageous fees and it doesn't do any harm. I was interested in the summary on the last page and when I'd read it I managed only a one-syllable word.

We found Henry Snape to be an endearing person, completely without guile and possessing an excellent attitude. However, we cannot recommend him for the post you wish to fill because he is simply not intelligent enough. The position as you have described it requires the salesperson to undergo in-depth product training, also the keeping of sales records, the control of credit and so forth. Snape would not be able to handle the work. With his Intelligence Quotient (see page IV, para c) we are of the opinion that his present job is his optimum level.

Not intelligent enough! Now, how did I miss that? I pulled out the notes I had made on Henry after my interview with him as well as the application form he had filled in. Now with hindsight I saw the childish handwriting, the poor spelling, the lack of any sentence structure. My notes had emphasised what a nice person he was, how well he would get on with our customers and his obvious honesty. I had been blinded by his good points; I had missed the one thing that would have knocked him out of consideration even if he had had wings and a halo. Damn!

Then the phone started ringing, fax copies began hitting my desk like snowflakes, D-M wanted my presence in his office in ten minutes, the Credit Department threw out two orders, the factory foreman came up to complain about salesmen barging into the factory, and Gaddafi the office cat deposited a dead mouse under my desk.

After a month's leave I was back to normal.

January

5 Friday

End of the week, and what a week. Mind you, everyone seems to feel it's been that sort of week at the end of every week. Haven't yet made up my mind about the two new sales people and D-M will start getting impatient at any moment. My week has been taken up mainly with setting sales quotas, and if there is a hell and I end up there, my job will be setting sales quotas for all eternity.

What happens, and it happens every year, is that as National Sales Manager I have to produce a sales forecast for the year ahead. I have to do this in November because our fiscal year starts on 1 February. I also have to produce a *five*-year forecast, but this is a grotesque piece of nonsense which should get me the Nobel prize for imaginative fiction, and Lord knows why the company insists on it. How do I know how much we will be selling in 1996? I don't know what our sales figures will be next *week*, and nor does anyone else.

Anyway, it is the year's forecast which is the important one. I get as close as I can, building in such variables as new products to be launched during the year, expected opposition activity, economic trends in the industry and the country, add a heartfelt prayer to St Jude, patron saint of hopeless causes, and bung it at D-M.

The Board then looks over my figures, sneers, chucks them in the fire and gives me another set of figures showing what it thinks I should sell – and in fact what I better *had* sell if I want my family to go on eating. Perhaps they don't actually consign my figures to the flames, but their figures are always different from mine and – surprise, surprise – they are always higher than mine.

I then have the job of, first, trying to talk the figures down with D-M, which usually doesn't work, and then – and this is the headache – of spreading the total quota around the members of my sales force.

One of the things that makes this exercise such a swine is the temptation to consider the capabilities of the salesman when awarding individual quotas. I tend to say, 'Well, Desmond has that territory and he always seems to be able to pull something out of the hat when we really need it. I'll up his figures a little more than Sandy's because Sandy falters when the chips are down.' That's the temptation, and I have spent most of the week fighting it and reminding myself that the quota always goes to the *territory*. It is based on the potential of the territory, and not the expertise of the salesman. Any other practice can only lead to disaster.

Well, they are all set and the letters have gone out to the salesmen, which means that next week I'll start getting the screams of outrage and agony. That, and the business of hiring the two new salesmen, has made this a hell of a week.

This is a three-drink evening.

January

9 Tuesday

Had my usual fight with Dorcas which I never win. I once instructed her never, under any circumstances whatever, to let me leave a letter unanswered, or at least unacknowledged, for longer than forty-eight hours. It seemed a good idea at the time; well, it is a good idea, but there are times when I wish that I had never thought of it.

She walked into my office this morning with her book, sat down and said, 'Now we do letters, yes?'

I said, 'Now we do letters, no. Dorcas, I am up to my ears in work. Tomorrow.'

'Tomorrow you will be up to your ears in letters. We do them now.'

I said, 'There are only three or four anyway. They can wait.'

She said, 'There are thirteen and they will not wait a split moment longer.' She had even looked in my dictation file and counted them.

I said, 'As your employer I hereby rescind the instruction regarding letters having to be answered within two days. That policy now falls away. It no longer exists. It is null and void. Go away.' She turned to a new page in her book and tapped her pencil against it. 'You damned Hungarian peasant, bugger off!'

'I am a damned Hungarian aristocrat and I will bugger off when we have done letters.'

'All right, Dorcas. You win,' I said wearily.

When we had fought our way through the dictation she nodded in approval, smiled and said, 'There! Do you not feel much better now?', as though I was a child who had just choked down a dose of revolting medicine.

I have already said that Dorcas is indispensable. It isn't true because no one is indispensable, but I would be in the most awful trouble if she left me. I say 'left me' instead of 'left the company', because our relationship is such a personal thing that it does seem as though she is working for me and not Hutton Horner.

I met a manager at a convention once who gloomily wondered how his secretary was 'fouling things up' in his absence. I asked why she should be fouling things up at all. 'Don't you trust her? Isn't she competent?'

He said, 'She is a good shorthand-typist, she can always find things in the files and she keeps my appointments straight. What else do you expect a secretary to do?'

I was amazed. 'What else? Why, just about everything. Look,' I said, 'here I am, away from my desk for three days. In that time I confidently expect that my secretary will go through my mail and answer routine letters, signing them on my behalf. She will pass any enquiries and problems on to people who can handle them, check that they have indeed been handled and make a note to tell me about them. She will receive any callers and, possibly, be able to deal with them. She will work closely with my Sales Correspondent on all matters concerning the sales force, check expense accounts, call reports, customer complaint forms . . .'

He put up his hands. 'All right, I get the picture. Do you really expect her to do all that?'

'Of course I do! When I am not there, my secretary is an extension of me, and the only things she can't handle are policy matters – staff problems which only I can handle – that sort of thing.'

He said, 'You keep her darned busy while you're away.'

'No, I don't. She keeps *herself* busy. She says she would die of boredom if she wasn't allowed to do those things. What it means is that when I get back tomorrow I shall have a small list of things which she has left for me to do because only I can do them.' I said, 'Tell me, what is your secretary doing for these three days?'

He looked irritated. 'Doing her nails and telling people that I'm away until Thursday.'

'And what will your desk look like when you get back to it on Thursday?'

'I won't be able to see my desk because of the heap of paper on it!' he snarled.

'I rest my case,' I said smugly.

There are managers who won't delegate because they seem to feel that unless they hug every bit of responsibility and authority to their bosoms they are not earning their salaries. It seems that they have to swim around in a sea of paperwork or they think they are cheating the company.

My mind works the other way. If I find myself doing routine work which Dorcas or Dicky could easily do, *then* I reckon that I am not earning my salary. It's a simple matter of arithmetic: I earn more than they do, therefore an hour of my time costs more than an hour of theirs. Thus if I do work which they can do, we are over-engineering the job. We are opening cans of beans with a scalpel, painting the garage with artists' oils, cracking peanuts with a sledgehammer.

There's another way of looking at it. I have always felt that an employee's value to the company is in direct proportion to *how far ahead he or she has to look* in order to do the job properly. It is necessary to keep the factory floor clean, but the men who sweep it don't usually have to look ahead any further than the next shift. A factory foreman has to look much further ahead – perhaps several weeks, to make sure that he will have enough stock of copper nitrate, brass bars, glass fibre or packing material on hand. The plant engineer is looking two years ahead to when he will need a new assembly line for that rotary cultivator they will be manufacturing them. And so on.

Dicky is looking about six weeks ahead to the start of the new sales cycle. Dorcas has her eyes four months into the future because the expense budget is her baby and she is determined that we will not exceed it by one five-pence piece. I am looking at least a year down the road on some things and even more on others. (Supposedly, five years for the long-range forecast, but I put that together using a pair of loaded dice and my aunt's old Ouija board while I say the alphabet backwards.)

So if a person's job is more important the further ahead he or she has to look, it follows that if long-range people are spending too much time on short-range work then something is wrong.

Which takes us back to Dorcas. She came into my office once when I was checking expense accounts, which is a god-awful job and about as inspiring as counting the fly specks on a light bulb. She said, 'Why are you doing that?'

I hadn't known Dorcas for very long then and I thought, boy, I've got a right one here. I said, 'Because if I didn't do it the whole sales force would go mad and start having lunch at the Dorchester.'

She said, 'No, I mean, why are *you* doing it? Why can't I do it? It doesn't look very difficult.' I stared at her.

So now I hardly ever see the expense accounts. Occasionally Dorcas will bring one in and query an unusual expenditure and I'll either approve it, in which case she wants my initials on it, or I'll throw it out, in which case the offending salesman will get a curt note from Dorcas. From what I hear around the sales meetings, the boys fear her more than they ever did me. The whole point is that checking expense accounts is *now* work, and people in management positions should be more concerned with *tomorrow* work.

MEMO TO ME: When you find yourself doing *now* work, ask yourself: 'Couldn't someone else do this?'

January

12 Friday

Four of the sales team happened to be in the office at 5.30 this evening, and when I walked through on my way to the car park they grabbed me, held me down, put an Uzi machine-pistol to my head, and bound me with chains so that I was completely helpless.

Well, perhaps they didn't do all those things, but the result was that we ended up in *The Marquis of Granby* on the corner – a pub which will go out of business if Hutton Horner ever moves its offices.

The result of that was that I got home nearly two hours late and in no condition to eat dinner, which in any case, as Annabel has pointed out, is now inedible. She has gone into her sewing room and it will be well into tomorrow before she starts speaking to me again.

Sometime in this diary I shall go into the dos and don'ts of a manager getting slightly sloshed with his team, but not tonight. Right now I'm going to take something fizzy and go to bed. Sorry for the irregular handwriting, diary.

January

17 Wednesday

I'm sitting with the diary open in front of me and I don't know how to start this entry. I'll put it down just as it happened.

Yesterday Michelle Sherborne our PRO phoned through and asked if I could give her half an hour today. I don't know Michelle very well because in my job I don't have a lot to do with Public Relations, but I said, 'Sure. Make it the end of the day, say 4.30.'

I've never had much of an opinion of PR, which has always seemed to me to be a part of the company designed to get its good parts into the public eye while keeping the bad parts carefully hidden. So you get the boss to give a cheque to an orphanage and get his picture in the papers doing it, but you make sure nobody breathes a word about the mercury you are dumping in the rivers which is producing frogs with two heads.

Anyway, Michelle turned up on time bringing into the room a smell of Chanel number something, and dressed as though she was going to a Belgrave Square cocktail party after work. It seemed that she had a real problem. A women's magazine called *Her* had phoned asking what Hutton Horner was doing about pollution, and didn't it bother us that our products were contributing to the rising pollution problem? Michelle had stalled the enquirer but she wanted answers, and Mac McLeod, our Factory Manager, was on leave, so could I help?

I gave her a cigarette and a light. There is a way that a woman accepts a light, by putting her hand completely over yours to steady the flame, and looking up into your face. So far I had seen this happen only in old movies with Charles Boyer and Claudette Colbert, and it was a surprise to experience it in my own office.

I moved back to the other side of my desk out of range. 'Well, in the first place a lot of people say "pollution" when they really mean "littering". The smoke from a diesel truck with worn fuel injectors is pollution; the mess that people leave around the Serpentine on a Bank Holiday is littering.' Michelle nodded and made a note on her pad. I went on. 'As far as our factory is concerned you would have to talk to Mac, but I understand that it is a very clean operation and has never had any headwind from the factory inspectors or health people.'

Michelle said, 'I see. But I think *Her* magazine is concerned with what you call littering. What *about* those chip packets and yoghurt cartons and fruit juice bottles in Hyde Park? *Her* magazine's point is that we make them, so we should somehow be concerned with cleaning them up.' She made a face. 'Not very logical, I know, but what should I tell them?'

We spent some time discussing the problem from different points of view – educating children about using litter bins, informing the public that most plastics are biodegradable and are not going to foul up the planet for the next thousand years, and so on.

When we had finished and she had promised to show me the article she was going to write for *Her* magazine, it was 5.40. She said, 'Oh, I'm sorry, Tom! I've made you late.'

I said, 'No problem. I often leave later than this.'

'And do you always go straight home?'

I looked at her. She was smiling very slightly. Wait a minute . . . *wait* a minute! What the hell was going on here? I said, 'Yes.' I remembered last Friday with the boys in the pub. 'That is, unless something comes up.'

'And could something come up this evening?'

'Er' . . . I felt like a callow schoolboy. 'No. I have to get home.'

She reached up and squeezed my arm. 'Pity. Some other time then, Tom.'

I drove home in a daze and I'm still in a daze. Annabel noticed it as she notices everything, and at dinner she said, 'And when do you think you will return to planet Earth, O famous space traveller?'

I said, 'Huh?' (My conversation today hasn't been scintillating.)

'You were a million light years away, love.'

So, a very attractive woman makes an unmistakable and fairly heavy pass at me. I have a marvellous family and my marriage works very well indeed, both in and out of bed. All the same, by golly . . . all the same . . .

I went into the bathroom and looked at the face I carry around all day. It's a thirty-six-year-old face and there are times when it looks every day of it. Hairline back about half an inch from where it was ten years ago, and a few strands of grey. Faint beginnings of bags under the eyes – Annabel says they look slightly dissipated and very sexy. I smirked at my reflection. Of *course* I won't get involved with Michelle. I love my wife and, anyway, it's a basic axiom of surviving in the business jungle that you don't fool around with the staff. As someone has said, 'Don't ever crap on your own doorstep – you will keep stepping in it.'

Still, it does your ego no harm to know that you've still got something. You are still smirking, buddy – go and suck a lemon.

January

22 Monday

I got out of bed today thinking, 'Oh-oh.' Funny, isn't it, how you wake up sometimes knowing that you don't want to get out of bed, but not knowing why. Then you lie back and think for a moment and you remember. What I remembered was that when I left the office on Friday I promised myself that on Monday I would make a decision about the two sales positions, and here it was – Monday.

When I got to my desk I pulled out the reports from the selection agency as well as the application forms from the seven hopefuls – now six, since Snape the Naval PT instructor was no more – and my notes on the interviews. I looked at all the bumf spread over my desk. Poop. Perhaps I should pop along to Cyril Headley and talk it over with him? No, Cyril's job as Personnel Manager finished the moment he handed me the list of 'possibles' which he had screened from all the applications for the jobs.

What if I took it all into D-M and asked his advice? Forget it; he would stare at me with that distant look and tell me that he had the utmost confidence in my judgement. That's what he would say but what he would mean would be, I pay you to make these decisions yourself, so don't come to me with every little problem. And he would be right.

My problem. My decision.

I spent pretty well the whole morning on the six applicants. There was no contest as far as one of them was concerned; his report was very positive and this was backed by my own remarks on his application form. I recalled his interview well and I remembered that I particularly liked his easy manner. I had noted down, 'Could deal at any level of buyer.' I was sure that he would fit into the team. Right, Mr Brian Hook – welcome aboard.

It was the second slot that was the bastard. The agency reports gave me two possibles, both with a lot of good things going for them. They were K. Wittenham and W. Carlton, and it seemed that either would fill the slot adequately. To be picky, Carlton had an edge on Wittenham in the agency ratings.

I would have come down on the side of W. Carlton without any further thought, but one thing was making me pause. I chewed the top of my ball pen until it shattered and left my mouth full of pieces of plastic.

The trouble was, the W in W. Carlton stood for Wendy.

Am I a male chauvinist? I sat at my desk staring at the report on Wendy Carlton and asked myself if it was at all possible that deep down, unadmitted, even unaware, I carried the old shibboleth of man being the provider and woman the home-maker and child-bearer.

I looked through her application form again. 'Age – 31.' Very good age; old enough to have lost a few illusions and young enough to be able to adapt to new circumstances. 'Marital status – divorced.' Also good. Well, all right, that sounds heartless and callous, but while I'm sorry her marriage failed it does mean that she doesn't have a husband who will expect her to be at home with supper on the table when he turns up at six in the evening. Also, and this has happened, you train her, supervise her, put her into the field and bingo – she turns up one morning and says, sorry, but her husband has been transferred and of course she has to up sticks and go with him: a lot of time, energy and money down the drain.

'Dependants – none.' All right, so there were no children from the marriage. Good from the company's point of view again. I'm not against children – two of my best friends are children – but I can imagine that if Annabel had a job and Angie woke one morning with a raging temperature and spots all over her tummy, Annabel would forget the job and not leave her daughter's side until she was better; and while that is natural and admirable in a mother, it isn't much help when you need to make eight calls on customers that day.

I sat back and thought of the interview with Wendy Carlton and I had to admit that she had come across very well. She wasn't a first prize in the beauty stakes – rather prominent teeth which she tried to hide by continually pulling her upper lip over them, and an uninteresting sort of hair style – but she was immaculately turned out, she was a good listener, she was bright, intelligent and articulate. I was impressed by her self-assurance.

Thomas Liskeard, you should be ashamed of yourself. I have just read through that paragraph again and I can't believe I wrote it. It is patronising and arrogant. Would I comment on a male applicant's teeth and hair? Of course not. As I notice now, even my written notes on Wendy Carlton are condescending.

I left my desk this evening having decided not to hire Wittenham. The first thing I must do when I get to work tomorrow is phone Wendy Carlton and tell her that she has just become our first saleswoman.

A small voice is saying, 'Proud of yourself, Liskeard? A few minutes ago you had decided against her because she was a woman. Now you have decided for her because she is a woman. Whether she turns out to be a good choice or a bad one, those are both wrong *reasons*.'

Oh, shut up. I'm tired and I'm going to bed.

January

23 Tuesday

I got Dorcas to write letters to the unsuccessful applicants. I suppose I should have phoned them and told them the bad news but I ducked out of it; it's not a nice job. At least I got the news off to them as soon as I had made up my mind – perhaps they were considering other jobs and it's not fair to keep them hanging on.

I had a home number for Wendy Carlton; I couldn't very well phone her at her work and leave a message to phone me. I called it and got her answering machine. I left my name and both my office and home numbers in case she didn't catch it until the evening. Brian Hook had already asked that I didn't phone anywhere but wrote him a letter instead in the event that he was a successful applicant, so that was no problem. Mrs Carlton phoned back just after lunch so she must have gone home at lunch-time. I said, 'I'm sorry we have taken so long about it but I would like to offer you the job you applied for.'

She said, 'Oh'. Nothing else, just 'Oh'.

I said, 'That is, if you still want it.' It didn't sound as though she was very keen.

She said very quickly, 'Yes, of course! I want it very much, and thank you!'

'You sounded uncertain.'

She said, 'No, it wasn't that I was uncertain. It's just that I didn't expect to get the job.'

'Why not?'

'Because at the interview you seemed . . .' she hesitated. 'You seemed to be against the idea of a woman in your sales force.'

'Oh, not at all!' Gawd love us, perish the thought. 'What gave you that idea?'

'Well,' she hesitated again. 'When I was waiting for you to see me I asked your secretary if there were any women in the Hutton Horner sales force and she said "No, not one." I hope you didn't mind my asking her.' Dorcas and her big mouth, although to be fair, what could she have said?

I said, 'No, of course we have nothing against women; it has just happened that way. Perhaps you will start a trend.'

We arranged that she would resign from her present company tomorrow and call me as soon as she knew when she could come to us without leaving her present company in the lurch. I liked that. Most people, when you offer them a job they want very much, will just walk out of their old company and to hell with any problems they may leave behind, so long as they give the minimum legal notice, no matter how good the company has been to them in the past.

I popped into D-M's office and told him which two I had chosen. It has been some time since he had a look at the application forms and my reports on the possibles, but he never forgets anything and he remembered the two. His only comment was, 'A woman at last? Are you mellowing, Tom? No longer a male chauvinist?'

I am getting *tired* of that word!

January

31 Wednesday

My God, a month has gone by already and I haven't yet settled down after my leave. What I have got to decide and quickly is the what, where, how, when and who of the sales conference. I have actually left out the most important question of all, which is why? Why have a sales conference at all? And saying 'Well, because we have one every year' is a bloody weak answer.

I jotted down some reasons to justify having an annual get-together of the sales division of Hutton Horner. In no special order the list came out like this:

1. To introduce new products to the sales force.
2. To inculcate and/or regenerate a team spirit.
3. To get across new policies and procedures.
4. To let the sales people have a chance to get gripes, problems and grievances off their chests.
5. To show them new sales promotion and advertising material.
6. To present awards for good performance and explain the new year's incentive plans.
7. To show the top brass what a hell of a good Sales Manager I am.

I dictated a memo to Dorcas listing the first six of these points as justification for holding a conference. The seventh point is of course not mentioned to anyone, not even Annabel. It is true that a successful sales conference can be a very good showcase for the Sales Manager, and it does no harm to remind senior management that this is *my* team and without it and me the whole of Hutton Horner would grind to a halt and then what would pay for the petrol for D-M's Bentley?

Of course, a sales conference which turns out to be a disaster is equivalent to a death warrant for the Sales Manager, no matter whose fault it was, so I shall be planning this one with the same care and attention to detail as a coronation.

February

1 Thursday

Michelle Sherborne got through to me on the intercom today. She wants to come and see me tomorrow to discuss the article she has written for *Her* magazine. 'I'd appreciate it so much if you would check the technical bits, Tom.'

I said that Mac McLeod was back from leave now, and suggested that he'd be better. It didn't work.

'Oh, I just can't relate to Mr McLeod, Tom. We have a *communication* problem.' I thought, I bet you do, if you hold his hand while he lights your cigarette and squeeze his bicep as you did mine. As I hesitated she said, 'What about 4.30 tomorrow, just like last time? The week is winding down by then and we shan't be disturbed.'

I said, 'Oh, fine. 4.30, then.'

'Looking *forward* to it, Tom.'

I put the phone down and said, 'Hell's bloody bells!' Dorcas happened to come in at that moment and her eyebrows asked a question. I said, 'Not you, Dorcas. Put Michelle Sherborne down for 4.30 tomorrow.'

It was probably only my imagination which saw a sceptical look on her face as she left the office. 'With all pleasure,' floated back over her shoulder.

Easy now, Liskeard.

February

2 Friday

Michelle turned up sharp at 4.30, just as Dorcas was leaving for the day. I was in the outer office and this time I didn't imagine the raised eyebrow on my secretary's elegant face, as she took in the flame-coloured blouse with two top buttons undone. She wrinkled her nose at the perfume, said her good-nights in a distant tone and left me alone with Michelle.

I got the trick with the hand when I lit her cigarette, but then Michelle became very businesslike and produced some sheets from a slim briefcase which turned out to be the article she had written. 'Don't be afraid to tear it to pieces,' she said. 'I'll just sit back while you read it.'

I quickly saw that it was competent writing. Without being too much of an advertisement for Hutton Horner, which *Her* magazine would never have gone for, Michelle had managed to convey that it was companies such as ours which really cared for the environment and which were spending money on making sure that people knew about recycling and reducing littering. I finished it and said, 'Great. It strikes just the right note.'

She was delighted. 'Do you really think so? I'm so glad! Isn't there anything you can suggest to improve it?'

'Not a thing that I can see. Oh, one small thing: you have called them "Ultra-Violet Preventors" and it should be "Inhibitors". That's all I can see.'

She got up and leant over my shoulder to see where I meant. I looked up and discovered that the flame-coloured blouse was gaping open and that she was not wearing one damned thing underneath.

Hell! It's not something you are faced with every day in your own office. I sat back with a jerk and she was looking straight into my face. She said, 'I have a bottle of the most incredibly delicious sherry in my flat and it is only ten minutes from where we are at this moment. Take it as thanks for reading the article.'

I said – and I had to clear my throat – 'Thanks, Michelle, but I can't be late this evening.' The wrong thing to say, damn it. Tell her to get off your case, that you are not available. She smiled slightly. 'All right, Tom; the sherry will keep. I promise you, you won't be sorry.'

I drove home trying not to think of flame-red blouses gaping invitingly. I opened the front door to be greeted by the sound of Angie bawling and Pete shouting that it wasn't his fault. Annabel was bending over trying to sort it all out. Her face was red and her kiss was automatic and her greeting perfunctory. She was wearing a grubby T-shirt and faded jeans and her hair was coming down. She smelt of fabric-softener.

For a traitorous minute I thought of the incredibly delicious sherry, not ten minutes from my office.

Hell and damnation! I picked Angie up and did a 'This is the way the ladies ride' until her tears disappeared. Then Pete wanted to show me what he claimed was a vole's house in the stream near the church, and when we got back home Annabel's hair was in place and she was wearing a white polo-necked sweater and lilac stretch pants and smelt of bath salts and she had made us martinis.

Suddenly, incredibly delicious sherry was a long way away.

February

5 Monday

Nearly got fired today. Well, that's much too dramatic, but I did stick my neck out and it could have been chopped. I had a talk with D-M about the conference and it took most of the morning. Big question – where? I suggested that we take the whole bunch over to France and hire an old *château* for the three days. I've been getting some direct mail about it and I thought it would be something new and exciting for the team. D-M turned it down flat with no discussion. I tried to tell him about the special deal being offered which meant that the whole thing would cost less than taking the team to the Isle of Wight, say, but he wouldn't even listen.

Do I ever turn one of the my men down with a flat 'No' and without allowing him to get a single word of explanation across? I suppose I do. Sometimes everybody who is in charge of somebody says, in so many words, 'This is the way it is going to be. Why? Best reason in the world – because I say so.' I think the subordinate will accept it, so long as it doesn't happen too often. He understands that it is going to happen from time to time, and as long as his relationship with his boss is such that in the normal run of things he can say his piece and that piece will be *listened* to, no great harm is done by the occasional, 'Shut up and do it my way.'

I didn't really expect to get away with my *château*, but I thought it was worth a try.

Then I won a point. D-M wanted to bring everybody into London. 'We'll save a lot on hotels because many of the delegates and most of the speakers live near enough to go home at night.'

I knew I had to stop that idea right away. 'D-M, one of the main ideas of a conference is that the team gets together after the day's work and renews friendships. Also, the London people would hate the fact that they are going home to help bath the children and fix the leaky tap in the kitchen, while their out-of-town colleagues are sitting around getting mildly pissed and having a good time.'

D-M looked surprised. 'Oh, you think that's important, do you?'

I was emphatic. 'Very important. Do you know what they talk about over a couple of beers after a day in the conference room? Oh, sure, they swap a few blue jokes but they actually talk *business*. They compare notes about problems, products and customers; they give each other ideas – it's one of the most important spin-offs of a conference. In any case,' I said, 'just being away from their wives for a couple of days is a morale booster for some of them.' This was positively Machiavellian on my part because D-M would also be coming on the conference of course, and it was said in hushed tones that Elizabeth Dunsby-Martin was a grim-faced female with a heart you could store frozen food in. Perhaps D-M had her in mind because he brightened up and said, 'Fine – let's take them somewhere away from it all – not France,' he said quickly, 'but somewhere.'

That settled, we got going on the agenda and here again I had trouble. D-M wanted the same sort of thing that Hutton Horner produced every year, which was a dreary procession of the top executives standing up and telling the salesmen how hard they would have to work in the year to come in order to keep the company solvent. At last year's do I had still been a salesman and I had sat through it all, and I was not going to let my people be exposed to it all over again. I crossed my fingers and put my head on the block.

'D-M, these are my salesmen we're talking about. I have to keep them motivated through the year. Now, if we are going to have the same sort of meeting we had last year then I'd rather we forgot about the whole thing right now.' I expected him to interrupt but he merely sat back with his fingers laced over his MCC tie.

'Last year you made the welcoming speech. This consisted mainly of telling us that although sales figures were up, profits were down, and that this state of affairs was unacceptable. D-M, I must tell you that your speech set an unhappy tone for the whole of the meeting. We salesmen thought that we had done a pretty good job over the year, and we had expected some pats on the back instead of words like "unacceptable". Also, we didn't see that the fact that profits were down had anything to do with us.'

I stopped, feeling that I'd probably said too much already. D-M didn't say a word. His mouth might have been a little tighter than usual but he just looked at me. I thought that I might as well be hanged for a sheep as a lamb. Carry on, hero.

27

'Then Don Thorpe stands up and puts the whole team to sleep by talking about cash flow and similar exciting subjects. Then Mac McLeod stands up and complains about salesmen making promises to customers about early delivery dates. Then Paul Hornsey spends ages telling us how hard the job of Credit Manager is and how much harder we salesmen are making it for him.' (I felt like a smoke but D-M was a non, and I knew that the crystal ashtray on his desk was for important customers only.) 'The point is, D-M, not that all that stuff isn't necessary; it *is* necessary. Salesmen mustn't pre-empt Mac's delivery dates. It is true that when salesmen don't give full credit information it makes Paul's job impossible. But what salesmen don't like is having to sit and listen to all that *without having their say.*'

D-M frowned. 'That's not quite right, Tom. There was a question period after each speaker, and the meeting was thrown open to the floor.'

I shook my head. 'D-M, every single speaker ran over his allotted time, so the moment he sat down we had Don standing up, looking at his watch and saying, "Well, we are running late and it's time to break for tea, but are there any questions?" Now, nobody is going to keep the whole meeting from having its tea and pee break by asking a question under those circumstances.'

'What do you suggest?' asked D-M. The tone was neutral; I didn't know how far I was from busking for a living on the Underground.

I took a deep breath. 'I want a tight rein on every speaker – he stays within his time-slot with no overrun. I want a Chairman, *not* from senior management, but from the sales force itself; each session to have a new Chairman. It will make the sales force realise that this is *their* conference. I want plenty of time for questions and a chance for people to submit written questions before the meeting. Then I want selected members of the sales force to speak for oh, ten or fifteen minutes on some aspect of their selling jobs, with time for participation from the floor. I want somebody – not me, I'm their manager – to stand up and tell them that they had done a helluva good job in the past year, because they have.' I paused. 'D-M, I want my team to walk out of that conference feeling *better* than when they walked in; last year they felt *worse*.' I sat back and awaited the hurricane.

D-M surprised me, as he often does. 'All right. All that makes sense. We have made mistakes in the past. Do you think that senior management should attend at all?'

I was astonished; it was the last thing I expected from him. I said,

'Heavens, D-M, of course you must be there! If you don't attend and participate, they will feel that the meeting isn't important enough for you to bother with. It's your being there that makes them realise that you are aware of the part they play in the success of the company.'

He said, 'Very well. Let me see a rough agenda in due course, and we'll think about a venue.'

Sitting here writing this I realise again what a good manager D-M is. He chops you into little pieces when he thinks you need it but he does *listen*.

MEMO TO ME: Learn from your boss, Liskeard. When your people are talking, even when they are saying something you don't like the sound of – *especially* then – *listen* to them!

A worthwhile day.

February

7 Wednesday

I wish I was better at what the professors call inter-personal relation-ships. I don't handle people very well, which is a hell of a thing for a manager to say. Oh, I'm all right in most situations, I suppose, but every now and then some confrontation comes up where I seem to play it badly.

Today I had Ken Milburn in for a chat about his sales figures. More than just a chat, actually, because the printout shows a nasty downward trend in his sales volume when his colleagues are mainly showing a slight increase.

Damn it, all I did was show him a graph of his figures compared with the rest of the division and he started crying. I mean real blubbing – tears rolling down! What do you do? Lend the man a hankie? Pretend he got something in his eye? I sat like a fool, not knowing where to look, and mumbling, 'Take it easy, Ken.'

Well, eventually he got himself more or less together. He said, 'I know that my work is terrible, Tom, but I'm going through a very bad time right now. Joanne says she is going to leave me, and I c-can't . . . I c-can't . . . ' Off he went again, tears like rain. I tried to place Joanne – she had to be his wife – and I had a vague recollection of a dim-looking female at the last company outing. I thought uncharitably, 'My God, she's nobody's first prize. Who is it that wants to throw her across his saddle and gallop off into the sunset?'

As though he had read my mind Ken said, 'There's – there's nobody else. She just says that she's getting nothing out of the marriage. She says I'm *dull*.'

I looked at Ken. I'm not proud of the fact that my first thought was 'well, hell, chum – you *are* bloody dull.' It wasn't a nice thing to think and I would never actually have said it, but it was true. Ken

Milburn is a character who simply doesn't have much character. He's a pastel-coloured sort of person. Five minutes after he's left the room you can't remember a single word he has said. Weak tea with lots of milk in it, that's Ken.

However, none of that mattered at the moment. The thing was that poor old Ken was in trouble, and what was I to do? I did not see that there was a single thing I could do that would help him, but he had different ideas. To my horror, he saw me as a sort of marriage counsellor.

'Could you come home with me and talk to Joanne? Please, Tom. There's no one else I can turn to.'

Jesus Christ, I thought, I don't get paid enough for this sort of nightmare. While Ken looked at me hopefully with his eyes brimming with tears, I pictured the scene in his living room: Ken crying, me asking Joanne to give him another chance, Joanne saying, 'But he's so dull!' Me saying, 'Well, okay, maybe he is dull, but think of all his good points, such as – come to think of it, such as what?' Impossible.

I said, 'Ken, old chap, I can't do that. This is a very personal thing; I just can't intrude on your private life. You and your wife will have to talk this out between you.' I searched for something else to say. 'Would you like a couple of days off, to be at home with Joanne?'

'No thanks, Tom,' he said miserably. 'That would make it worse. Joanne says that she can't stand to have me around the house.'

Eventually I managed to get him on his way. Dorcas came into the office and found me staring at the wall. She asked, 'What troubles you?'

I said, 'Sit down. Let me bounce something off you.'

She said, 'I am wishing you would not use those hum words.'

'Buzz words.'

'Thank you. Buzz words. What is the problem?' I told her. Dorcas is so discreet she would make a Swiss banker sound gossipy.

'What should I do? Should I actually try to talk his wife out of leaving him?'

'In Hungary once a man was fighting with his wife. A cousin of mine tried to stop the fight.'

I said, 'What happened?'

'What happened was that the man broke my cousin's jaw and as he lay on the ground, the wife kicked him in his private parts. Stay out of it. It is not your business.'

31

When I got home this evening I told Annabel and asked her what I should do. She said, 'Stay out of it. It is not your business.' She also said, 'Joanne Milburn! She thinks that *Ken* is dull! Look who's talking.'

All very well, but one of my men is suffering and he was so desperate that he came to me for help. I'm going to have to think about this one. Perhaps it is my business after all: by coming to me, Ken made it my business.

There's nothing about all this in my job specification. Hell!

February

9 Friday

D-M phoned through first thing with what he obviously thought was a brilliant idea. 'What about Ireland?'

I was still fighting my way through my first cup of coffee. I said, 'Ireland?' as though he had said Outer Mongolia.

'For the conference!'

'For the – ' It dawned on me that he was talking about the venue for the sales conference. I said, 'Ireland? *Ireland?*'

D-M sounded enthusiastic. 'Of course! Pop across by *Aer Lingus*, take over one of those old country houses which are set up for conferences. It will be something different. What do you think?'

I thought it was a wonderful idea and said so. 'Good,' he said. 'I'll get my people on to it. Leave it all to me.'

I am only too delighted to leave it all to him and his people, which means that Evelyn Street, his secretary, will be cursing me and my sales conference. I put the phone down and grinned hugely. Not only was that one big thing that I could scratch off my list, but if the venue turns out to be a disaster, with a leaky roof, no electricity and poisonous food, it won't be me that roasts slowly over an open fire.

Isn't it odd that when the day starts out with one piece of good news, it seems to guarantee that other good things will happen all the way through the day? Or is it just that that first piece makes your attitude positive and this sparks off the other good things? Whatever, a very good day and a good end to the week.

February

15 Thursday

Didn't go near the office today – I should do this more often. Spent the whole day calling on customers with Reggie Plumstead of the Industrial Rigids division. I have wanted to do this for some time for two reasons; firstly, I wanted to get a closer idea of what the opposition is doing in the industrial field, and the best way to do this is to call on the customers themselves; secondly, I've been a little worried about Reggie and I wanted to watch him at work. He's a good man, a solid worker, but I had the feeling that when the time comes to tie the customer up with a signature on the order, Reggie freezes over the putt.

Encouraging to see that Privett Plastics, our major competition in the Rigids section, is still using the older type of injection moulding equipment. Reggie pointed out several instances where we got in ahead of them because our newer machinery produced a cleaner product from the mould. I told him that it was nice to see that we were on the ball but that he shouldn't get too complacent about it; in the plastics business, especially the high-tech side, new ideas come out every year, and we could find ourselves behind Privett with them using machinery which was produced after ours. Still, it's good to see that we are still ahead and I must tell Mac McLeod about it.

Reggie himself is not nearly as bad as I thought. He isn't an assertive salesman, though, and several times today I wanted to take over the presentation and close decisively. I didn't, of course: that's an absolute no-no in field training of a salesman. Do that and you destroy the salesman's confidence in himself. Worse, you confuse the customer, who thinks: who *is* the salesman here? Much better to chat to Reggie after the call, suggesting a different way of going about it. Reggie takes supervision very well; he's keen to improve. As to his choking up when the time comes to close, I must remember that in

Rigids each order has a very big potential. It isn't like Retail Flexibles where the order can be worth as little as £50. An order taken by Reggie could be worth £10,000 spread over two years, and it's not unnatural to be a little nervous about it (so long as the customer doesn't see the nervousness, of course – a nervous salesman produces a nervous customer and no sale).

On the whole I'm happy with Reggie Plumstead, but it needed the trip into the field with him to decide this. More of those trips with other team members, and soon!

And having written that confident, positive piece of prose I realise that it can't be done. I have twenty-three sales staff reporting directly to me. There are about 220 working days in a year. If I spent only one day every three months with each person – four days a year, which isn't enough – it would chop 92 days out of my year, leaving me with 128 days to do my job. Impossible.

I read somewhere that a manager can handle no more than ten sales people reporting directly to him. It is very probably true. Have I been neglecting my boys in the field? How long is it since I took a trip up north, for instance?

MEMO TO ME: Think seriously about getting D-M's thoughts on appointing two Area Managers. (He will probably go straight up through the ceiling in a sitting position).

February

27 Tuesday

Spent part of the day getting things ready for Wendy Carlton and Brian Hook, the two new sales people who are due to arrive on Thursday. These are the first additions to the sales team that I have hired off my own bat, and I want things to go right. I remember what happened when I joined the company and I don't ever want any of my people to go through that bloody shambles.

I got there bright and early on the first of the month and nobody had remembered that I was supposed to be starting that day. Bert Corley, the Sales Manager at the time, had even forgotten my name! When he realised that I was there and waiting to have something done about me he began rushing around like a blue-arsed fly saying things like, 'It's really the worst time – I'm so busy now – what shall I do with you?' Then he had a bright idea. 'Have a look through these product catalogues, er . . . Liskeard. Sit down over there and I'll be back soon to answer any questions.'

He wasn't back soon. I looked through the catalogues five times. I even read the printer's name on the back. Some time during the morning someone poked their head into the office and, bless their heart, arranged to have a cup of tea sent in. Three hours later Bert Corley returned. He said, 'Well! Have you been through the catalogues yet?' I said I had – I didn't say how many times. 'Good! Well, any questions?' I said, 'No, no questions.' How could I ask questions? I didn't *know* enough to ask questions.

That rather floored Corley. He drummed on his desk. 'Well, what are we going to do with you now?' He looked at me as if he confidently expected me to tell him. I felt like apologising for the fact that I had turned up that morning and proved to be such a nuisance to a busy manager. I felt like saying, 'Why not slash my wrists and be done with it?' I was disgusted with the whole business. He ended up

36

putting me at the desk of the Sales Correspondent who viewed my arrival with ill-concealed hatred. I learned later that he was in the habit of doing crossword puzzles between spells of work, and I had innocently put a cramp on that activity.

When I got home that night and Annabel asked how my first day had gone I said, 'I may have made the biggest mistake of my life, joining that disorganised rabble.'

Well, it turned out that they weren't really as disorganised as all that, they just didn't have a proper induction programme for newcomers, and it is so important that the first impression the newcomer gets is a positive one. Bert Corley was a good Sales Manager, too; this turned out to be about his one and only blind spot.

Whatever Wendy Carlton's and Brian Hook's destinies in Hutton Horner are going to be, whether they become Managing Directors or are fired in disgrace, their first few days in the company are going to make them feel welcome and completely catered for.

I reminded D-M of their forthcoming arrival and he said, 'Good. I'd like to see them, shake hands, chat for a moment. Would that be all right?'

I said it would be excellent and he told me to bring them through to his office some time in the morning. I thought about that and said, 'D-M, I'd rather not shepherd them into your office. All that panelling and leather and wall-to-wall stuff will be rather too much for them. Would you mind coming to my office to meet them? It would make it less formal.' For a moment I thought I'd blown it. Who was I to tell the boss to present himself at my office?

He nodded. 'Much better idea. Much better. Say sometime between oh, ten and half-past? Get Mrs – ' (Very few people can pronounce Dorcas's surname, and D-M isn't one of them.) 'Get your secretary to phone through and I'll come running.' D-M always surprises me.

Well, that's all done and ready for Thursday.

February

28 Wednesday

Every now and then every Sales Manager in the world wonders what evil demon possessed them to accept the promotion from the ranks of sales representative. They were happy as a salesperson; at the end of the day they walked away from the job and relaxed. They didn't take it all home in their head and they didn't have a care in the world. They earned enough – in fact, if they were on any sort of commission basis they might have been pulling in more than their Sales Manager. At one time or another every Sales Manager says, 'Why don't I just chuck it all up and go back to carrying a sample case and an order book and live the simple, happy life again?'

Today was one of those sort of days. D-M had a cold word to say about East Anglian sales; Paul Hornsey rocked in and went on and on about a possible bad debt for £1,800; I spilt coffee over three letters which had to be retyped and that put Dorcas in a mood; I realised that my smoking rate had crept up above the absolute maximum which I had set myself; some clown scratched my car in the car park; I raised my voice to Dicky Bird and had to apologise because the problem hadn't been his fault – one of those days.

I have just told Annabel that I feel like packing it in, taking on a few lines and going into the selling business as a freelance. She smiled and kissed me and said, 'Well, it's worth thinking about, darling. Bad day, was it?'

I realise that I tell her the same story about twice a year. She said, 'Come what may, time and the hour runs through the roughest day.' I suppose that's a quotation; it's what you get for marrying an intellectual. Anyhow, I hope it's right.

March

1 Thursday

Every now and then I do something which turns out exactly right. It doesn't happen all that often and when it does it makes up for a lot of the times when things *didn't* go right.

Brian Hook and Wendy Carlton turned up early, as I knew they would, and I had made sure that I was there before them. Dorcas was at her desk, too, but then she always is there half-an-hour before time. I sat them down at my desk and gave them each a typed programme of what they would be doing for the next two weeks, showing where they would be and who they would be working with. Also a 'family tree' chart of the Sales Division with all the territories and who handled what and where. Dorcas produced coffee while we were going through the programme.

I had decided not to take them through the whole office introducing them to everyone. It doesn't work, because after the first ten people it becomes a sea of faces and it is impossible to remember people's names and positions. They will find out who everybody is as they go through the different departments in the course of their training programme.

I gave Dorcas the nod to phone D-M and he came in and was introduced. He chatted informally to them, perching himself on the corner of my desk. He does this sort of thing very well; he had taken the trouble to read up their CVs and he talked to both of them about their previous jobs and, in the case of Brian Hook, he asked him what he sailed in – I had forgotten that on Brian's application form he had put it down as one of his hobbies. He was gracious to Wendy Carlton and said he hoped that her joining the team was the beginning of a trend towards hiring women as sales people, which may have been a dig at me. After telling them he was sure they were in good hands (mine) and thanking them for the opportunity of this introductory meeting he left. Courteous to a fault, my boss.

I took them to the boardroom and their training proper began. First, Don Thorpe's assistant took them through the whole business of pension plans, annual leave, and the various dos and don'ts of company policies and procedures – such as don't ask the company for an advance on your salary because you won't get it (except that a lot of people do ask and often *do* get it). Then Paul Hornsey gave them a talk on credit policy. I have sat through Paul's talk before and it always manages to sound threatening. Not his fault, I suppose. He has the worst job in the company. Who'd want to be a Credit Manager?

Then Mac himself came up from the factory which surprised me; I had thought he would send one of his assistants. He turned out to be terrific, talking about how important it was for Production and Sales to work closely together, how his people could help the sales force if they were given enough lead time, what could be done and what was absolutely impossible. Then I'm darned if he didn't take them out of the boardroom and give them a tour of the factory – something I hadn't dreamt he would do. He even phoned this afternoon and said how he had enjoyed talking to them, and what a good idea it was to show them the ropes as I had been doing.

Although I didn't sit in on all the different sessions I was looking at my watch all day to see where they had to be next and who I would have to remind that it was their turn to take over the new boys – or rather, the new boy and new girl; I am going to have to get used to not thinking of the team as 'my boys'. Dorcas, as usual, was fantastic at keeping calls and callers off my back while I got Brian and Wendy (we had got to first names by then) through the programme.

At the end of their first day they were back in my office with more Dorcas coffee. (One day that woman will kill me with caffeine poisoning.) I asked them what their impressions had been so far. They looked at each other and Wendy said, 'We've been talking about it, and we agree that we are very impressed. The fact that a special programme was drawn up just for the two of us, that busy executives have spent time with us, that everything has gone so smoothly – if this is the way this company operates, then we think that we are lucky to be working here.' Brian nodded emphatic agreement.

This evening Annabel met me with a warm kiss and a cold gin and tonic. 'How was your day, love?' She doesn't usually ask me that.

I said, 'Fine! Couldn't have been better.'

'Still feel like chucking everything up and going on your own?'

'What?' I said. Then I remembered my remark yesterday. 'Oh, hell, no! In any case if it weren't for me, Hutton Horner would go straight to the dogs.'

'Of *course* it would,' she said.

Smart woman.

March

7 Wednesday

Went to a cocktail party put on by our advertising agency. Because so much of our business is industrial instead of retail, we don't do enough advertising to warrant having a full-time adman, so advertising is one of the hats I wear. I fully expected to be bored stiff and I decided to have one quick drink and leave, but as it happened I met another Sales Manager who turned out to be very good value to talk to. Ray is in the publishing business, and he opened my eyes to some fascinating aspects of selling books. This is the marvellous thing about selling; in so many ways it is the same no matter what you sell, and in so many ways it is completely different, one industry from another.

I was delighted to hear that he agreed with me on one secret of selling which I am always trying to get into my salesmen's heads. It is simply this: *call when other salesmen don't.* Ray said that when he was selling to all the railway station bookstalls in the London area, he would try to hit them as early as possible – 6.30 or 7.00. By the time the other sales people arrived on the scene at 8.30 or 9.00, Ray had tied up a good deal of the bookstalls' spending money in his products.

I could tell him the same story about my early days when I sold to pharmacists. Now, ask a salesman in the drug trade and he will tell you that it's no good calling on a pharmacist before 8.30 in the morning, because the shop isn't open yet. Absolutely right, but the interesting thing about a chemist's shop is that the door is made of glass: you can see through it. I wonder how many times I've stood outside a pharmacy at seven in the morning and knocked on the glass door. The shop isn't open, but the pharmacist is usually there all right, hidden away in the dispensary. The pharmacist looks up and there I am, making 'coming in' gestures through the glass. What

better time to sell to them? No customers interrupting your presentation, no telephones ringing – and no other sales people. It was
refreshing talking to another old campaigner in the selling business.

Then he said, 'Tell me, Tom; suppose, when you were a salesman,
you had a morning when everything went right and you were pulling
orders like a whale sucking in plankton. You get to lunchtime with
your order book bulging. What would you do?'

I said, 'I'd probably skip lunch break altogether and keep on calling
until my last customer shut up shop for the night; when you're on a roll
like that you dare not stop!'

He said, 'And suppose you got up one morning and started calling
on customers as usual and absolutely nothing went right, so that by
lunch-time you not only had an empty order book but you had the
feeling that you had wasted the whole morning; what would you do?'

I said, 'I'd go home, get changed, and do fifty miles on my
twelve-speed. Hell, in that frame of mind, if I called on any more
customers I'd do more harm than good.'

He laughed. He said, 'You're right, of course. But do you know that
when I ask my sales people the same two questions they say exactly the
opposite? If they have had a fantastic morning selling, most of them
admit that they would take it easy in the afternoon and probably knock
off early. If they have had a terrible morning, they say that they would
battle like mad in the afternoon to try to make it up.'

Well! Thank you, Ray, for putting something into words which I
have always known and practised, but never thought of as a selling
philosophy.

It's all a matter of attitude, of course. With a really successful
morning behind them sales people will make their afternoon calls with
a winning attitude; when their morning has been an absolute disaster
they call on customers in the afternoon as though they are bringing
news of the start of World War III. In those circumstances I don't want
my sales people within a hundred miles of a customer. Nor, of course,
do I want them in a pub drowning their sorrows, or at home getting
under their partner's feet. The best thing they could possibly do is
something very physical – play a few hard sets of tennis, run fifteen
miles, work out at the gym – anything to get their mind off the mess
that was theirs this morning.

And I would want them to tell me about it. If they pretend that they
have spent the whole day in their territory and I find that they have
been fishing, they will be in more trouble than they would have
believed possible.

Perhaps I should do the same thing? There are times when I feel that I'm doing more harm than good sitting at my desk, so why not go and work up a sweat around Green Park? Not so easy as it was when I carried a briefcase and smiled at receptionists. Now I have to soldier on, even when I feel that the angels are dumping on me that day.

Well, Liskeard, you are pulling in what many people would think is an exorbitant salary with all the perks. Whatever made you think that the job was going to be easy?

March

5 Monday

An age-old problem cropped up again today, as it does about once a year. Pat Swallow came into my office looking irritated. Pat is one of my best salesmen in the Central area, and when a good salesman wants to get something off his chest then his manager listens. He said, 'I called on the buyer of Triple-Six Stores yesterday and as soon as he saw me he started crapping on me because of a wrong delivery last week. I didn't know what had hit me because he didn't *get* a delivery last week. Then I realised that he wasn't talking about me at all, it was Derek Warnaby's problem. Derek had sold him something which had been screwed up somehow, and I was getting headwind because of Industrial Flexibles.'

I said, 'Yes, I know it happens sometimes.'

'It happens too damn often, Tom. The trouble is that when I told the buyer that it wasn't my division, he really got annoyed. He said, "It's all the same company isn't it? Why are you trying to dodge your responsibility?" Tom, I don't need that sort of hassle in my life.'

I could sympathise with Pat Swallow. I had faced the same sort of problem when I was in the field. It comes from a basic sales policy about which every company has to make a decision: do we division-alise our sales force or not? Which simply means, do we have a sales person selling the entire range of our products, or concentrating on one *type* of product?

It is a very important question, and there are strong arguments for and against each side.

At Hutton Horner our sales people are divisionalised. This means we can give them more in-depth knowledge of their products because they are dealing with a very limited range. They are specialists – almost, in fact, sales engineers – in that they can give their customers

45

technical advice on the use of their products and really get 'inside' the customer's working situation.

The down side of this policy is first that because they don't handle the whole range, they can miss some applications for other products. A salesman can have been selling one-pint plastic bottles to a customer for years without realising that the customer is an absolute natural for waterproof film. Also, and this was what Pat was bitching about, you can have two or even three Hutton Horner salesmen calling on the same customer, each one selling different types of product, which can lead to the sort of confusion which Pat encountered. 'No, thanks; your man has already been here today,' is the frustrating reaction which the divisionalised salesman can get from customers.

We could have the whole sales force selling the whole range of products. The first good news would be that my expense budget would drop by about one-third. Far less company car mileage, far fewer calls – Don Thorpe would never stop smiling. No customer confusion, either, with only one Hutton Horner salesman calling in that territory. Another big point would be that because the sales force handle all our products they would have their eyes open for applications for all those products.

Why don't we do it that way, then? Well, the problem is that we sell some fairly sophisticated products. We sell garbage bags, certainly, and there isn't very much to a product like that – no special expertise is required to flog ten thousand packets to a chain store. But what about the factory engineer who wants to know right now, this instant, at what stage our EB-400 film loses memory-stretch and becomes dead-stretch? The engineer is busy setting up equipment and wants the answer without a salesman looking blank and promising to come back with the information tomorrow.

So our Retail people call on supermarkets and other retail outlets while the Industrial people have government bodies, factories, mines and so on as their customers. We even find it necessary to split these divisions into Rigids and Flexibles, so our people really are specialists. This causes problems, but at least we can't be accused of the old 'Jack of all trades and master of none' problem.

I don't know. I've chewed this over with the sales force and no easy solutions have come up. They are not stupid and they can see the pros and cons of both sides. Some of them like the idea of generalisation – handling the whole ball of wax. They like the feeling that they and only they represent the company in that particular territory, with no interlopers and no poachers screwing up their customers.

On the other hand some of them hang on fiercely to the specialist idea. They like to feel that they are the experts in their field, that technical people ask them for technical advice – that they are the 'consultants'.

I've discussed it with D-M and he isn't interested in changing. 'It works well as it is,' he says. 'Let's not change the winning game.'

I agree with him. I *think* I do.

March

13 Tuesday

Weirdest thing. Here I am sitting in my own living room making notes about the sales conference. I take a look across the room every now and then because Annabel likes to take little bird-like sips of a weak Scotch and water through the evening, and occasionally she needs topping up. I saw that her glass was empty and gave her a refill, and then peered at what she was doing. It looked like completely meaningless letters and numbers and squiggles on a piece of paper.

'And how are you getting on with your Hindustani lessons?' I asked.

She said, 'Urdu, you ignorant peasant. Hindustani was *last* month.'

I said, 'All right, I'll buy it. What is that stuff?'

'I'm about to make some school shirts for Pete,' she said. 'I'm planning the sewing, as anyone with a morsel of sense could see.'

'*Planning* the sewing?'

'Certainly. First I do it in my head and then I put it down on paper.'

I was lost. 'But what do you mean, planning the sewing? Don't you have a pattern?'

'As it happens, with these shirts I don't have a pattern. But even with a pattern you have to do things in *order*. If you don't do things in the right order you can really get into a mess.'

I said, 'Well, I'll be damned!' I walked over to my chair and brought back what I had been working on. 'You see this?'

'It looks like a chart of some sort,' said Annabel.

'It is a chart. It has the rather pompous name of Critical Path Analysis. I am doing it for the sales conference. Roughly, what it means is that certain things have got to happen in the right order and at the right time. The venue has to be booked by that date so that the

48

flights can be booked by *that* date. The advertising displays have to be ready by *then* so that they can be sent to the venue by *then*.'

Annabel isn't usually interested in the ins and outs of my job, and I am eternally grateful for this, because it means that she doesn't pump me about my day when all I want to do is forget it. But now she was interested. She looked at my chart and then at her letters and numbers. She said, 'It's the same idea.'

I said, 'It is; and I do mine for the same reason you do yours. Am I right in assuming that if, for instance, you sew the . . . oh, say the peplum in before you sew the gusset, you've got a problem on your hands?'

Annabel looked pained. 'You could use a quick course in sewing, but yes, that's roughly what I'm guarding against with the plan.'

'How long have people been doing this sort of planning?'

'From the time when someone made the first needle out of a dinosaur's wish-bone, threaded it with the guts of a pterodactyl and sewed the skin of a sabre-toothed tiger together to make a loin-cloth.'

Blow me down; there really *is* nothing new under the sun.

March

15 Thursday

D-M stuck his head into my office this afternoon. I don't know where he had had lunch but it wasn't at the Temperance League. Perhaps when I am Managing Director I'll be able to have three-hour lunches where the wine flows like coke. I'm not knocking my boss; for all I know, he might have been buttering up someone important to the company.

What he wanted was to tell me a story he had just heard; he couldn't wait to get my reaction to it. It seems that in the marketing company of one of the people D-M had lunched with, there was a salesman of thirty-five years' standing. Very friendly character, loved by his customers, seemed to like being just what he was, a salesman. He was coming up to his sixty-fifth birthday, which would normally have meant retirement, but the management wondered if he would like to carry on for a few more years, since he was fit and healthy and had no dependants. 'Perhaps,' they thought, 'we could cut down his territory a bit so that he doesn't have to work so hard. Let's put it to him.' So they said, 'Herbie, how would you like to carry on after normal retirement age?'

Herbie thought that this might be a good idea.

His Sales Manager said, 'You see, we could give you a smaller territory and take some of the load off your shoulders – make it a half-day job. How about that?'

And Herbie said with a smile, 'Mr Elton; I've been doing a half-day job for thirty-five years!'

D-M laughed like hell at his own joke and left. I sat there laughing. Then I suddenly stopped laughing.

MEMO TO ME: I know you do it regularly, but go over all salesmen's call reports again, and see if any of those guys out there are doing a half-day's job for a full day's pay.

50

March

19 Monday

I wasn't going to write anything in the diary today – nothing much happened at the office – but I have just had an interesting phone call right here at home. It was the top man from the recruitment agency which we had used to get Wendy and Brian. I thought it odd that he should phone me at home, but I thanked him for the reports and hoped that he had received our cheque.

He said, 'I expect so, Mr Liskeard.' He was probably far above anything so low-class as Accounts Receivable. 'But this call concerns you. I should very much like to meet you again and discuss something which could be of great interest to you.' He paused. 'To you personally; not as Sales Manager of your company.'

I said, 'Oh, yes?' (Snappy comeback, that.)

'Could you have lunch with me in the next few days? Not in a restaurant, I think. We have a small place in the office here. I'd appreciate it very much.'

Well, how about that. I said, 'Very well; what about Thursday?'

'Excellent! Say, 12.45? Looking forward to it, Mr Liskeard.'

I put the phone down. I knew that Annabel wouldn't ask who I'd been talking to because she never does. One of her many virtues. I said, 'Well, how do you like that? The head-hunters are after me.'

Annabel looked blank. 'Head-hunters? With poisoned arrows? Darling, have you been working too hard?'

Basic rule of good communication: don't use jargon which is familiar to you, but may not be to the listener. Odd how easy it is to forget that a term like 'head-hunters' still means to most people little brown men with bones through their noses and shrunken heads stuck on poles! I said, 'Sorry. In the business jungle a head-hunter is a company which specialises in finding people for jobs, and they work by approaching people instead of waiting for people to apply for the job.'

51

'And they have approached you?'

'Yes. Your husband is in great demand, so let's have a little more respect around this dump.'

Annabel ignored my pleasantry. 'What company is it that wants you? Is it one of Hutton Horner's competitors?'

I said, 'Ah. One of the rules of this head-hunter game is that they don't tell you the name of the company until you are practically in bed with them. That's why they use a middleman. First you play a little footsie with the middleman.'

'And are you going to play a little footsie?'

'Thursday lunch will see me pick up the handkerchief which they have discreetly dropped in my path.'

'Why? Aren't you happy where you are?' Annabel asked.

I said, 'Yes, I'm happy where I am. But I would be stupid not to take a peek at what is being offered, wouldn't I? It costs me nothing and it can't hurt.'

'Will you tell Mr Dunsby-Martin what you are doing?' Which shows how little my wife knows – or cares – about business.

'Hell's bells, no. This is all very hush-hush at this stage. In any case, nothing will come of it.'

'Then why bother to go?'

How on earth do you explain? But she wasn't really interested and I didn't try.

Head-hunters, wow! Liskeard, you may be better than you think you are. We shall see on Thursday.

March

Do people change? Really change, I mean; change their characters or personalities or psyches or whatever. I used to think they didn't. I thought that people got more experienced, developed, became sophisticated perhaps, but that they did not change the essential person.

After this morning I'm not sure.

When I took over as Sales Manager from Bert Corley he sat down with me and gave me a complete run-down on each member of the sales force. Now, I had been one of the crowd and I knew most of them by sight and some pretty well, but Bert gave me his opinion of them from the point of view of a manager, not of a fellow-worker.

Looking back now I see that this was not a good idea, but I was green in the job and I didn't realise it at the time. I should have stopped Bert the moment I realised what he was doing, because what happened was that I ended up with *his* ideas about the men, which meant that I was starting with his prejudices. It wasn't long before I saw that if I was to work with my new team – new to me, that is – I had to sweep away everything he had said and start with a fresh page for each man.

One of the team that Bert had shaken his head over was Dan Lathom. He said, 'Watch this man very carefully, Tom. He is substandard in just about every aspect of his job. If I had stayed here another three months I would have fired him, but I knew I was leaving and I thought I would give him one more chance with a new manager.'

Thanks very much, I thought, so you chickened out and left me with the shitty job of firing him. Bert went on, 'You can see what you think, but I have done everything I can and my feeling is that Lathom is a no-hoper.'

With a character reference like that I naturally watched Don not only very carefully, but also with something of a jaundiced eye. Bert Corley had given this dog a bad name and I was perfectly ready to hang him. However, I was determined to give him more than a fair chance. If I had to get rid of him then so be it, but it was going to be on my evaluation, not Bert's.

I went out with Don, calling on his customers, I did a couple of informal appraisals on him, I went over his sales figures with a fine-tooth comb and through his paperwork as though they were the Dead Sea Scrolls. After two weeks I was prepared to go along with Bert's evaluation of him, and the only thing which kept me from firing him was the fact that I had been in the saddle for only a fortnight, and I didn't want people to think that I was suddenly drunk with power and starting to chop heads off willy-nilly.

Then Dan Lathom changed. He changed from a taciturn, almost surly individual into a bright, pleasant and participative person. His figures began a steady upward climb, his admin. work improved, even his car, which when I had first gone out with him looked like something dug out of Pompeii, now gleamed and sparkled.

None of this happened overnight, but three months after I had taken over, Dan was fifth from the top of a team of twenty-three salesmen. He was an asset at sales meetings, with good questions and high participation. I hadn't a clue what caused this metamorphosis, but I certainly wasn't complaining. My appraisal ratings on him were right out of sight compared with the first ones I had done on him. I gave him his due share of congratulations and of course he began appearing on the monthly and quarterly awards lists.

It was only this morning, though, that I thought, damn it, I am going to find out what happened to turn Dan Lathom from a lemon into a star. He had come into the office to ask permission to give one of his customers a display stand. 'I know that according to the rules his throughput isn't high enough yet to warrant it, but he's as keen as mustard, he loves our products, and he has promised to give the stand prime space in his shop. What do you say?'

I said, 'Screw the rules. Go for it.'

He said, 'Hey, thanks. I'll go and give him the good news right now,' and he made to leave.

I said, 'Do you have a moment, Dan? Something I want to ask you.'

'Of course. What's the problem?'

'There's no problem; not now, anyway. But this time last year *you* were the problem. Do you realise that two weeks after I took this job on you were this close,' I held my thumb and forefinger half an inch apart, 'to being given the chop?'

He nodded. 'I was expecting every day that you would call me in and fire me. I was pretty awful, wasn't I?'

I said, 'Awful doesn't begin to describe what you were, and not only your performance; your attitude could have been used to poison cockroaches.'

He frowned. 'Yes, I gave you a hard time.'

I said, 'Never mind me; I didn't expect the job to be a bed of roses. What I want to know is, what *happened*? What turned the miserable bastard of a year ago into one of the best men in the team?'

Don said, 'Well, *you* happened.'

'What? What are you talking about?'

'You took over from Corley and from that time things started going right for me.'

I didn't understand. 'But I didn't do anything special. In fact, I was quite prepared to get shot of you.'

'I know; I could see that you weren't very impressed with me, the very first time we went out together.'

I felt I had to admit something. 'Of course it's true that my feelings about you were at least partly influenced by what Bert Corley had said about you.'

'I suppose so. You should have heard what I had to say about him in those days.'

I said, 'But Bert was a good Sales Manager. I was on his team too, you know.'

Dan said earnestly, 'Tom, I know he was good at his job. There was just something between us and don't ask what it was because I don't know. Perhaps we just started off on the wrong foot, and I'm quite willing to say that most of the fault could have been mine. Anyway, nothing that I did was right in his eyes, and I eventually got the feeling well, to hell with you, you bastard, and I simply became bolshy.'

I said, 'And when I came along?'

'Well, as you know I was still bolshy.'

'I know you were,' I said with feeling.

'Yes. But you went out with me for a day and although I know I didn't do well – hell, I wasn't trying very hard – at the end of that day we had a cup of coffee and you made a few remarks about my performance.'

55

'I did?' I didn't remember that.

'Yes. Now in the same circumstances Bert would have found nothing but faults, and as I say, there were plenty of faults to find. But you didn't criticise. You pointed out a few things that I could have done differently and you actually praised the way I had handled one of the customers.'

'I remember something. I don't think I went overboard, though.'

'No. But when I got home that night I told my wife about you, and she said, "He sounds like a fair person. It would be nice if he was able to say some more good things about you." I thought about that, and I decided to make you do just that. So you see, when you ask what happened, *you* happened.'

I said, 'It sounds as though your wife happened, too. She seems to be a clever woman.'

'Yes. I can't have been much fun to live with in my bolshy period.'

Dan Lathom *changed*. I would love to take all the credit for changing him but I think that something like that happens only when the person has it inside to change. What helped Dan to change was partly the *recognition* I had given him for something he had done competently. He called it 'praise', but I don't think that praise is the right word. You can go badly wrong with praise; it can sound patronising or insincere. It can even sound as though you want something in return. No, the word is recognition, and of course where we are heading for here is *motivation*. I've always felt that a lot of the so-called motivational techniques are just gimmicks. I'm sure that when someone does a good job and the boss says, 'Nice work, Andy; you did that well.' Andy is motivated as almost nothing else can motivate him.

Of course, it has to be genuine recognition of genuine worth. Any fool can go around scratching their staff behind the ears, handing out choccies and saying, 'Good boy, Towser. Good girl, Spot.' That isn't genuine recognition, that's flannel, and it won't produce motivation; it will produce contempt.

Do I recognise genuine effort enough? I heard a manager in another company say once, 'You have to be careful about handing out "Well done" and "Good show" too often, you know. Tell a person they're good and before you know it they are asking for more money.' My God, what an attitude!

The thing is that recognition doesn't have to be fulsome. My first job was working for a character who chewed railroad spikes and spat out iron filings. Tough he was, but always fair. His highest accolade was to stride past my desk, toss something I had done back at me and say, out of the side of his mouth and without pausing in his stride, 'Nice!'

What did I do? I hung my tongue out and wagged my tail in sheer ecstasy, because I knew that he never said anything he didn't mean: *genuine* recognition of *genuine* effort.

MEMO TO ME: *Recognise* more!

March

22 Thursday

Well, I went to lunch with the head-hunters. The top brass there are very urbane types and remembering what Annabel said, it was difficult to think of them with Afros and blow-pipes. I got the full treatment – introductions to Hamish someone and Douglas someone else and, 'Shall we toddle in for potluck?' Potluck was very smooth sherry while we chatted about Five Nations Rugby, about which I know little and care less. Then grilled trout with an almond sauce and a dry white wine with an expensive label, but which tasted sour to me; I like it a little less drought-stricken. Then a cheese board with cheeses I've never seen before; one was covered with what looked like a lot of grape pips. Glorious coffee to finish off; no liqueurs, I suppose to have heads clear for head-hunting in the afternoon.

The end of the sherry finished the Five Nations and then it was all business. There was a company which was looking for a General Sales Manager and my name had come up. No good asking the name of the company, but I did ask if it was in the same field as Hutton Horner. No, it was in metal, not plastics, but the concept was the same – containers, foils, packaging. The top man said, 'The customers are the same as yours, Tom.' We were Hubert, Hamish, Douglas and Tom now, very buddy-buddy.

Well, the type of company made sense. I didn't know the products but that wasn't as important as the fact that I did know the market. Perhaps these people, behind all the hunting prints on the walls and the bone china and crystal, were actually pretty good at their jobs.

I asked about the money. Except that you don't apparently talk about *money* to head-hunters, I was oh-so-tactfully corrected. 'The *package*, Tom, is really quite attractive, but what is even more interesting to someone as far-sighted as you is the future potential.'

Is that a fact now, I thought. I may be something of a peasant when it comes to a grape-pip cheese, but behind my ears there is not one trace of damp. In my experience, when someone tells me that while the *now* is pretty good, by golly the *tomorrow* will be fantastic, it really means that the now isn't all that marvellous.

So it turned out. The money – sorry, Hubert, the package – was not all that different from what I was getting now, and the car plan, pension and all the other goodies were also much of a muchness. I said so; there was no point in being coy. After all, I hadn't sought this pow-wow.

Hubert looked a little pained. 'Ah, Tom, but there will be a seat on the Board in the not-too-distant future for a man who proves himself in the position and Sales Director is a very different situation from General Sales Manager.'

Which sounded fine, but the same thing applied where I was; it was obvious that the next step up from my job was a seat on the Board, so long as I did the job properly for who knows how long. Also, I had already begun to 'prove' myself in Hutton Horner; I wasn't starting from scratch, as I would have to do in a new company.

Was I interested in taking this further? Possibly to the extent of meeting the CEO of the company in question? I said that I thought not. I was flattered at being asked, and thanked them for the time, but I was happy where I was. The atmosphere got a little cooler, but Hubert and Hamish and Douglas all shook hands with me and wished me luck. They even sounded as though they meant it; almost, anyway.

Over dinner I told Annabel about the lunch. She was more interested in the menu than the business; apparently what I had eaten was *truite amandine*. I said that I wasn't interested in changing my job for the one offered.

'But didn't they tell you the name of the company? How can anyone make a decision about changing to a new company if you don't know what you're changing to?'

I said patiently, 'That would be the next step, and they did offer an interview with the boss of the outfit. I said thanks, but, no thanks.'

Annabel said, 'I knew you wouldn't be interested in changing.'

'How could you know? I didn't think that I would be, but I didn't know for certain until I'd talked to them. You couldn't have known.'

'I know you, darling.'

Women.

March

23 Friday

Went to work today wondering if I should tell D-M about the head-hunters; I was sorely tempted to. It would do me no harm at all for management to realise that I was a much sought-after bloke, so take good care of Liskeard, stroke him now and then, and listen carefully when he talks.

Better not; it's a little too obvious.

Anyway, I told Dorcas, who would undergo a grilling by the Inquisition before she would let out my secrets. She was amused. 'They think you are a pretty good person, hey? I could have told them you were a pretty good person.' I smiled smugly. 'Almost as pretty good as you think you are.'

I stopped smiling. 'Go to hell, Dorcas.'

'Not now I don't go to hell. Now we do letters.' I sat down submissively and got out the letter file. Dorcas said, 'I knew you wouldn't leave here.'

I said, 'How could you know? You didn't even know I was going to see those people.'

'I know you, *liebling*.'

Women.

April

2 Monday

One of the sales training companies had phoned for an appointment and I spent most of this afternoon with them.

The whole business of sales training has been bothering me ever since I took over this job. What is the best way to tackle sales training? I don't mean product training of course, which is done right here in the company; I mean training in the art of selling. What should I do? Could I put together an amateurish sort of course based on my own experience in the field? Should I get one of the training companies and let them loose on my people? At the moment I tend to do it on an *ad hoc* basis; if I get a piece of direct mail advertising a course in Manchester, say, I send the four sales staff in that area on it. I knew that this wasn't a good long-term idea, and so I was prepared to listen to the gentlemen from Proselling PLC.

I started off not very tactfully by saying, 'You know, gentlemen, I have never been able to get rid of the feeling that sales training is something of a con.'

They weren't offended. One of them said, 'Don't bother to try to get rid of that feeling, Mr Liskeard. Much of the sales training being offered *is* a con.'

'Why do you say that?' I asked.

'Because most of it is public training. That is, it is offered to all and sundry, and the people who attend the courses will be exposed to a syllabus which has to be broad and vague, in order to cater for the different industries represented at the course. This means that most of the sales people won't be able to relate to the material of the course, because it doesn't deal with their specific selling situations.'

'Why can't the syllabus cover their situation?' I asked. But I felt that I knew the answer.

'Mr Liskeard, your people sell plastics. Now, isn't it a fact that your industrial sales people have a different selling situation from your retail people?'

That impressed me. These fellows had done some research on Hutton Horner before they had approached me. I said, 'Yes, they do. They sell different products from each other and they often sell them to different types of customers.'

'So in fact, to be really effective any training should take that into account,' said Tweedledum. (They looked just like twins, these two; short haircuts, button-down shirts, dark grey suits, black leather briefcases; clean-cut.)

Tweedledee said, 'In fact, it could even make sense for the two divisions to go through slightly different training.'

I said, 'Possibly so.'

'Then how much worse would it be if your sales people attended a course where they were sitting next to people selling window-cleaning services, night watch security, short-term insurance and hotel supplies?'

Dorcas brought in coffee, serving it with the grace of a countess, which, of course, she happens to be.

I said, 'All right, you've made that point. The best sales training must be in-company. Why shouldn't I go the whole hog and hire a full-time training officer, instead of using people like Proselling?'

Tweedledum and Tweedledee smiled in unison. Tweedledee said, 'That would be your ideal solution, Mr Liskeard. A full-time training officer would be one-hundred per cent involved with your people, able to build a course around your products alone and answerable to you for the success of the training.'

'It sounds as though you are trying to talk yourselves out of business. Tell me why I don't just hire this person, then.'

Tweeldedee said, 'Because you can't afford him.' Before I could react to this, Tweedledum smiled. 'That doesn't mean that this fine company doesn't have enough money to pay for a full-time training officer. It means that it would simply not be an economical proposi-tion for you. You have what – between twenty and thirty salesmen?' Another indication that these two had done their homework. I nodded. Tweedledum said, 'It isn't a big enough sales team to warrant the expense of a good trainer.'

'And he *must* be a good trainer,' his twin said. 'He would be responsible for all training and development of your entire sales force. You can't afford to have someone who became a sales trainer simply because he couldn't make a living as a salesman.'

Damn it, I thought that is what has always worried me about sales trainers; I just haven't put it into words.

Tweedlesomething said, 'You would have to pay a good, competent trainer somewhere between what you pay your best sales person and what you get yourself, Mr Liskeard. Now, that's just salary. Add to that office accommodation, use of at least half a secretary, company car and so on – the arithmetic is against you. Compared to what Proselling would charge you to run a complete training programme for your entire force, tailor-made to fit their precise selling situation, your sales trainer would be an expensive luxury.'

I acknowledged that what they had said made a good deal of sense. They tried to get a commitment from me to use their services. Well, that was all right; I wouldn't have thought much of them if they hadn't asked for the order, as it were. They got no commitment and it wasn't their fault. As I told them, 'The problem is that even if I was completely sold on using your organisation, and I'm not as far down the road as that yet, I simply couldn't sign anything right now for the best reason in the world; I don't have a budget for it. The odd bits of training I have used from time to time have been paid for by stealing money from my advertising budget. Before I even talk to you people again, I'm going to have to go to the front office for a training budget.'

At that moment I could have written their script, because I had used what in sales training jargon is called the 'third party stall'. I had said, in effect, that before I could give them the order I would have to bring another person into the decision-making. The classic counter to that is: 'Well, can't we see this other person with you?' They used it.

'That's understandable, Mr Liskeard. I wonder if we could help you when you talk to your senior management? There might be some questions which we haven't covered here today, and if we were there to answer them it could speed up the decision process.'

I grinned at the twins. 'Gentlemen, if all three of us walked in cold turkey to my boss man's office, the only thing it would speed up would be my leaving the company permanently.'

A good salesman knows when to stop pushing for a close, and to live to fight another day. They left, promising to phone me within ten days. When they were gone I did a bit of figuring. They had been very plausible about how much a full-time trainer would cost me but – wait a minute – they had compared his salary and other expenses with the cost of using their services, and it wasn't as simple as that. Anyone who would work full-time for me in a training capacity would be able to do a hell of a lot more than an outside training company. As I sit writing this in my diary, I can think of several ways in which a full-time trainer would be better than using the Proselling crowd:

1. He would run the sales training itself and, as Proselling has admitted, it would be completely oriented towards our products and selling situation.
2. He would be able to do the product training, which would be a big nuisance off my back.
3. All the records on each sales person's progress in training, their ratings in product knowledge tests, their appraisal sheets in field training – all that would be the trainer's responsibility.
4. The trainer could handle at least some of the field training. Not all of it, because I would always want to go out with the sales people, but I have already realised that I can't do it all.
5. He would do most of the induction training, so that I wouldn't have to run myself ragged getting the right people into the right places at the right times.

And looking over that list, I realise that I have been slightly conned by Tweedledum and Tweedledee. I may have something interesting to say to them when they phone in ten days.

I have a good mind to get Dorcas to type out the above list and to walk it into D-M's office. Of course, getting him to agree to my hiring another body will be like getting milk out of a duck, but I have a good case, surely?

April

4 Wednesday

I have been thinking all day about the five points I wrote down yesterday and I can hear D-M's reaction to them: 'Tom, it seems to me that the one person who would undoubtedly benefit from our getting this training person is you. You seem to reckon on them taking over a good deal of work which is surely the responsibility of a Sales Manager?' I can hear him saying it, and see him with those eyebrows raised and his fingers laced over his Guards Brigade tie.

And what would I say to that? Because deep in my heart I know that, in a way, he would be right. A trainer would take over a lot of work which I don't really like doing. I might as well admit it in these pages which no one else will ever see. I like my job, but I don't like *all* of my job; everyone has bits of their work which they would just as soon someone else did. The only exception I can think of is Dorcas, who seems to do everything from making coffee to cleaning her word-processor with the same serene attitude.

There's another thing, and it's only just struck me. Suppose I do accomplish a miracle and get D-M to agree to the trainer. Then five minutes after this person is established in his new office I ask D-M for permission to promote two of my sales people to the position of Area Managers, and hire two more sales people to take their places. I can picture it now. His eyebrows will shoot right up to where his front hair used to be and he will say, 'Tom. I have just taken on, at your earnest entreaty, an extremely expensive training person who will be doing a third of the work which I used to pay you to do. Am I to understand that the function of these two proposed – what? – Area Managers, will be to relieve you of the other two-thirds of your duties? With nothing whatever to do, Tom, will you not be terribly *bored*?'

At times, D-M can get heavily sarcastic.

Now, there's a perfectly sound argument to put up against all that, and some day I'll think of it. I have to be careful about asking for more bodies, even when I know they are necessary and that they will benefit the sales division and therefore the company as a whole. I could easily get the reaction: 'Bert Corley ran a perfectly successful and happy ship without taking on a lot of extra petty officers. What's the matter, Liskeard – can't you handle the job on your own?'

MEMO TO ME: Don't rush either the sales trainer or Area Manager ideas until you have your ducks very much more in a row.

April

5 Thursday

The usual cliché is that a man's wife is naturally suspicious of his secretary, and fears that, since they spend so much time together at work, he may become entangled with her in some way, if not directly sexually, then emotionally. It doesn't work that way with me.

Six months ago when I introduced Annabel and Dorcas at a company outing they immediately cottoned on to each other. Lord knows why this should be since there is a twenty-year difference in their ages, and their backgrounds and situations are so different. Anyway, they get on like a house on fire; they phone each other and natter – probably about me.

Last week Annabel said, 'Do you ever take Seraphita out to lunch?'

I was reading a Beatrix Potter book to Angie, and with any Beatrix Potter you have to keep the rhythm going. I said, 'What?' and Angie made a noise of irritation at the interruption.

Annabel said it again. 'Do you ever take Seraphita out to lunch?'

Ask any husband a question like that and I don't care if he leads the life of a saint, he will feel a stab of guilt. I quickly ran all the women I have ever met in my life through my mental computer and I couldn't find a single Seraphita. I said, 'I don't know what you are talking about. Who is Seraphita?'

Annabel said patiently, 'Your secretary. Do you – '

'My secretary?' I was flabbergasted. '*Dorcas?*'

'That's a stupid name for her. Seraphita is the nearest you can get to her Hungarian name.'

'Seraphita. Well, what do you know! I think I'll stick with Dorcas. What is all this about taking her to lunch? Why would I want to do that?'

'Because you should show her some appreciation occasionally,'

Annabel said coldly. 'What have you ever done to say, "Thank you for the wonderful job you do"? Have you ever given her a small present?'

My head was spinning. With feminine intuition, Angie had realised that the Beatrix Potter session was over and had left in disgust. I said, 'This is the wrong way round. Men are supposed to take their secretaries out to lunch and buy them presents and *hide* it from their wives. Why do you want to overturn an arrangement that has been going on for ages? Anyway,' I said defensively, 'I can't very well give her a present out of the blue and I don't even know when her birthday is.'

'It's August the 8th. Make a note of it. And take her to lunch – you could probably put it on your expense account anyway; it would make a lot more sense than buying lunches for your fat customers.' She started counting stitches out loud, which she doesn't do unless she wants to signify that the conversation is ended.

So yesterday I said to Dorcas – Seraphita, if you please – 'Wear your pretties tomorrow. You and I are going to shake the dust of this dump off our feet and have a lunch somewhere.'

If I expected her to be astonished or overwhelmed, I was disappointed. She smiled graciously and said, 'That will be lovely, Tom. Thank you. Where shall I phone for a booking?' The efficient secretary to her fingertips. I thought what the hell, let's do it in style, and told her to get a table at the Châtelaine. She pursed her lips. 'My goodness. We will cut a dot.'

'A dash.'

'Thank you. A dash.'

So today, bullied into it by my wife, I took my secretary to lunch. Dorcas wore a plain black dress with a single strand of pearls and, for the first time since I'd known her, some expensive-smelling but discreet perfume. She looked terrific and she walked into the Châtelaine as though she had come there only because the Savoy Grill bored her. Breeding shows.

We had a hell of a time. Dorcas nattered away to the maître d' in rapid French and he fell in love with her to the extent of more or less ignoring me until the time came to present the bill. We got back to the office at 2.40 and Dorcas thanked me very prettily and kissed me. I said, 'It's something we should have done long ago, and we'll do it again.'

I was in D-M's office later this afternoon and I told him what I'd done. I thought I might as well, since he was paying for the lunch. I said, 'Do you ever take Evelyn to lunch, D-M?'

'Evelyn? *Lunch?*' You might have thought that I'd asked him if the two of them ever attended a Black Mass together.

I said, 'You should, you know. Show your appreciation of the wonderful job she does for you.' I supposed that she did do a wonderful job for him; as far as I was concerned, all she did was keep me from seeing him when she thought he shouldn't be disturbed, and one day she and I were going to come to blows about that.

He said, 'Lunch? *Evelyn?*'

I left him looking bewildered. That's it, Liskeard; keep them hopping.

April

12 Thursday

The Proselling twins phoned yesterday, nine days after they had come to see me. They had promised to phone within ten days, and a good salesman keeps his promises. Of course, a clever salesman never *makes* any promises, as the old story goes. They didn't want my answer on the phone, they wanted to come and see me again, 'To show you something interesting which we neglected to mention on our last visit.' Standard selling practice: try not to get the prospect's decision on the phone, because it is too easy for them to say, 'Sorry, I've decided against it,' and put the receiver down. Try for a personal visit, then it's not so easy for them to throw you out.

I told them to come along. I wanted to see them again anyway; I hadn't made up my mind about an agency versus a trainer hired by us, and there were a few things I wanted to take up with them.

They turned up on the dot as expected; a good salesman is punctual. They waited for permission to sit; a good salesman is courteous. Tweedledum opened a briefcase which must have cost three times as much as mine and pulled out a piece of paper. 'We thought you had a right to know our track record before you made any decision, Mr Liskeard. These are some of the companies for whom we have run in-company training over the past three years.'

The list was impressive. Some multi-nationals, some smaller ones about the size of Hutton Horner, but all good names. I looked for the names of plastics companies, but either they hadn't done any work for outfits in our field or they had been tactful enough to leave them off the list. I said, 'Yes, you have made the point that you are not amateurs. You know, gentlemen, since we last spoke I have been doing some thinking, and I have still not given up the idea of hiring my own man to do training for us instead of using some outside company.' I said, 'You have shown me a piece of paper; here's one of

70

mine.' I passed across the list I'd made out. 'Those are some of the things which a good man could do for me and which you could not.'

They read the list attentively, taking their time and nodding their heads. They passed it back. Tweedledee said, 'We can't argue with that, Mr Liskeard; it's absolutely right. Two things, though. Do you realise that most of our clients – those companies you saw on our list – use us in spite of the fact that they already have sophisticated and effective training departments of their own? We fill a gap which is simply not economical for a company to fill themselves. Second, a good training man could certainly do those things you have listed. A *good* man; and that may be the problem.'

'How do you mean?' I was interested. If there was a problem here then I wanted to know it.

'We agreed the last time we were here that only a good person is worth considering, and that anybody not out of the top drawer would be a disaster.' He leaned forward. 'Mr Liskeard, where will you find such a person? It's not like hiring a salesman, you know. A good salesman is not easy to find these days, and a good trainer is ten times more difficult, believe me.' He smiled. 'We hire them and we know what rare birds they are.'

I said, 'What makes them rare birds?'

The other twin took over. (I would like to see these two do a vaudeville song-and-dance act.) He said, 'You find two types of people in training, neither of which you or we want. The first is the person who has a very attractive platform personality and is an excellent public speaker. The problem is that he has little or no practical experience of selling. You know, probably better than we do, that you can't fool experienced sales people; the moment they realise that the person behind the lectern is there because he has read a lot of books on the subject of selling but hasn't himself trod the pavements and knocked on the doors, they reject the course with contempt.'

I nodded. 'Right. Most of my people would see right through anyone like that and walk straight out of the room.'

'Just so. But there is a second sort of person who finds their way into the training business. They are the naturals, the ones who can go out and make a sale where there was no sale to be made. At some stage or another they decide that there is an easier and more pleasant way to make a living than rushing around in all weathers calling on people. Why shouldn't they work in a comfortable conference room? So they become sales trainers.'

71

I said, 'Fine! If you know someone like that send them along to me.'

A twin said, 'Never. If we sent them along to you, we would be doing you a very bad turn. Mr Liskeard, that person is a sort of selling freak. He will sell in spite of the fact that he breaks all the rules. Now that's fine for him but not for a sales person attending a sales course and looking for a track to run on in selling. That natural sales person doesn't have to bother with tracks, he simply takes off across country. But can't get his expertise across to others because the truth is that he doesn't know how he does the things he does – and in any case, he knows nothing about running an effective conference. No, sir; you don't want one of those.'

I sat back. I had to admit that what they said made sense. They hadn't finished. 'There's one more thing. If the person you hired really was as good as you need, he wouldn't be working for you. He would be working for us, because we can pay him more than you can.'

'Or, of course,' the other twin said, 'he wouldn't be working for either of us; he would have gone into business on his own as an independent trainer.'

We talked some more. I reminded them that I still had to sit down with my masters and get the authority for setting up a training budget. They understood, or said they did.

'You aren't simply buying a product here, Mr Liskeard. This is an important policy change for your company and it has to be carefully thought out and fully discussed. We'll be in touch, and thank you for your time and for your close attention to our presentation.' Good salesmen show appreciation for the prospect's time and they leave the door open for the next visit.

Out of all the talking and thinking I have done about this training business, I am sure of only two things; I could make a big mistake on this one if I took the wrong path, and whatever I do is going to cost an arm and a leg – probably mine.

April

17 Tuesday

Both the children have some sort of bug: temperatures, coughs, runny noses and, of course, waking up through the night. The moment she hears either of them wake, Annabel gets out of bed. I feel guilty about it. We have never discussed it, but it has always been understood that since I have to go to the office in the morning, reasonably rested and ready for a tough day, it is Annabel who attends to the children when they are restless at night, even if this means that she gets very little sleep.

The guilt feeling comes from the fact that I know very well that when I kiss her goodbye in the morning and push off to the office, I leave Annabel still holding the baby – literally, in this case. She still has all the housework, cleaning, washing and shopping to do; she can't turn over and grab an hour's extra kip, even if she had almost none in the night. She is on call twenty-four hours a day.

Another thing. That tough job I need all that sleep for – as any manager knows, whether or not they will ever admit it, the job isn't *always* as tough as all that. I leave Annabel with one foot in the washing machine, the other in the sink and both hands changing sheets on a cot that has just been sicked up in. I walk into my comfortable, air-conditioned office where my secretary brings me coffee and my Managing Director pops in, drapes himself over a chair and tells me what a hell of a good job I'm doing. I get home having had a really easy day, and let no manager tell you that they don't have easy days, to find that Annabel is so rushed off her feet that she hasn't even had time to make herself a cup of tea. I say, 'What did you have for lunch?' She looks at me blankly and says, 'Lunch? Oh, I was holding five safety pins in my teeth and I can only find four of them. I probably had the fifth one for lunch.'

For lunch I had a very nice *salade niçoise* and a cappuccino, and

73

suddenly I feel a right bastard. I can tell myself that it isn't my fault, that I have to go to work, that I can't just take time off because the children have tummy aches and my wife is overworked. I can rationalise it, but it doesn't make me feel any better.

There's another thing. I have arranged to go to Wales and spend three days and two nights there, calling on customers with David Lundy. I'm leaving tomorrow morning, and Pete and Angie are no better. Annabel hasn't said anything, but she knows as well as I do that the dates for this trip are not carved in the tablets that Moses brought down from the mountain. I *could* put the trip off, even though it would mean David phoning some big customers and postponing appointments. For me, the trip would mean that I would be free of the children's coughing and waking in the night, and I'm not proud of the fact that it would be a relief. But it's my job, isn't it, and isn't it Annabel's job to hold the fort while I'm out there doing it?

I read over what I've written and I stood up, went to the phone and called David Lundy in Cardiff to put off the trip for a week. Annabel was walking through and she heard the conversation. She put down the two hot drinks she was taking through to the children and put her arms around me and leaned against my chest.

Tonight if the children wake up I'll take my turn. I'm not a complete bastard, only say, three-quarters bastard; the other quarter is husband and father.

April

26 Thursday

Management conference in the boardroom. When D-M wants to get it across that there is a crisis of some sort, he calls for a meeting in the boardroom rather than in his office, even if there are only two people involved. This time there were all four of us – D-M, Don Thorpe for Finance, Mac McLeod for Production, me for Sales.

D-M opened it up. 'I've asked you all to be here because we have a situation which could use some constructive ideas and I'm hoping that with all of us contributing we might come up with an answer. The situation we have is in Production, so Mac, perhaps you would explain it to Don and Tom?'

Mac McLeod is a highly qualified man with all the AMIMechE's and so on behind his name. He's not a great talker, which makes some people think that he's a bit thick, and I get the idea that he doesn't mind that at all. I'm sure that it's just a front and Dorcas (how do secretaries get to know these things?) once told me that Mac is a sort of amateur authority on the writings of Walter Scott, which impressed me because I had read *Ivanhoe* as a set-book at school and I couldn't make head or tail of it.

Mac looked almost embarrassed. He said, 'As I've told Mr Dunsby-Martin' – Mac never called him 'D-M' – 'I have what I can only describe as a morale problem in the plant. It is not obvious and up to now it has not affected production, but I want to do something about it before it gets worse.'

Don Thorpe said, 'What are the symptoms, Mac? What are the men doing that worries you?'

Mac turned to me and said, 'Well, it has to do with your people, Tom.' Before I could say anything he held up his hand. 'Now don't misunderstand me. I'm not blaming Sales or anybody in it. It's true that sometimes a salesman will make a bit of a nuisance of himself by

75

coming into the factory and wanting his order moved ahead of everyone else's – '

Don Thorpe interrupted. 'D-M, wouldn't it be better if we simply made it clear to all sales staff that the factory is out of bounds to them?'

Damn you, Thorpe, I thought. First of all it is no business of yours and second, don't talk to D-M, talk to me. *I'm* head of Sales. D-M shot a quick glance at me before he replied; perhaps the same thought was going through his head. 'Not as simple as that. Sometimes a salesman has to work with Mac or one of his staff on a new product design. The salesman knows exactly what the customer wants and often a drawing doesn't give the whole picture.' Sucks to you, Thorpe.

Mac went on. 'But that's not the problem, or only indirectly. Take an example: I've got a good man, Albert Binley, a machine minder. He hasn't been his usual happy self in recent weeks and Ron Aston asked him if there was anything the matter. He thought there might be some financial trouble, or something at home, for instance. Albert said, "No, no problems." Then he said something about, "Must be nice to be swanning around all day in a company car, taking it easy and keeping your hands clean." As he said it he was looking at one of your boys, Tom, who had brought a colour sample in from a customer.'

I said, 'Now, wait a minute. That was Artie Watford and he had to bring that sample in; in fact, Ron Aston had asked for it specifically. And believe me, he was not swanning around; he was halfway through a very long day's work.' I was ready to climb into the ring on behalf of my team but D-M raised a finger to stop me.

'Mac isn't saying that Watford shouldn't have been there. This meeting is not for the purpose of complaining about the Sales Division or anyone in it.' He was right and I had gone off half-cocked as usual.

Mac said, 'This is a problem I have come across from time to time, not only in Hutton Horner, but in other companies I have worked in. The fact is that people who work in factories wear overalls, they get their hands dirty, they stand on their feet all day, they work in constant noise, they get hot in summer and cold in winter.' Mac paused, and looked at me. 'And there's another thing, Tom. I said that nobody is blaming your people for all this, but d'you know, salesmen can be very quick off the mark to blame us when we make mistakes – and we do, oh, yes, we do. But when we do a good job, do

76

they ever come in and tell us? That same Artie Watford came in and practically went down on his knees for us to get the Elstree order out three days ahead of the promised date because Elstree had suddenly run out of stock. We pulled out all the stops, turned the number three assembly line upside down, and we did it. We never heard a word from Watford, Tom or,' he cocked an eye at me, 'from you.'

I felt myself going red. I like Mac, we get on well together, and I admire the way he does a difficult job. What he had said was no less than the truth, and I didn't have a word to say in my defence. I said, 'Yes. You are right, and I'm sorry. I'm afraid that we are too quick with the kicks and damn stingy with the ha'pence. Point taken and it will change from now on.' I didn't like eating humble pie in front of D-M and even less for Don Thorpe to see, but what could I do?

Mac let me down easily. 'Och, Tom, I know that you appreciate what we do and sometimes you are too rushed to think of it. Don't worry about it.'

D-M breathed through his nose. 'In any event, that is not why we are here. I asked you to come in to see if there is any way we can help Mac. One thing we know for certain and that is that the fault does not lie in the factory itself. For three years in a row we have got that award from those Safety people, and they give it not only for safe conditions in the plant but for what one could call, oh, Human Relations, as far as the staff are concerned. Mac is to be complimented on his concern and regard for his people.' D-M leaned forward, and I knew that we were about to hear the real reason for the meeting. 'I have had an idea and I'd like your reaction to it.' (D-M never used terms like 'I'd like to bounce this off you' or 'Let's run this up the flagpole and see who salutes'.)

'Tom, how would your sales force feel if we asked them to take some of the factory people into the field with them for a day at a time?'

I looked at him. 'Do you mean, take them in to see customers?'

'That's right. Show them what the sales force does. Help them to understand some of the problems your people have out there.'

'There's another thing about this, Tom, if you agree.' This came from Mac, so D-M had aired the idea with him before this meeting. 'You know, my men make the products, but they don't often see them in use. It might give them a greater interest in their work if they knew what happened to the things they spend all day making.'

I liked it. I could see it helping to make for a better relationship between Sales and Production. D-M was looking at me. I said, 'Yes.

77

Let's go for it. There are one or two things to iron out, but I think the idea is terrific.'

Don Thorpe had to stick his nose in. 'How long will the artisans be away from the factory?' Bloody accountant's mind at work, of course. Translation: how long will we be paying a fitter, turner or toolmaker while he isn't earning any money for us? D-M made my day by saying irritably, 'Let's let Mac and Tom work out the details. They needn't concern us,' meaning, 'Keep out of this.' Thorpe's mouth snapped into a thin line and his ears turned pink. D-M said, 'Can we leave it to you two?'

Mac said, 'You can.'

I said, 'Fine.'

I'm seeing Mac on Monday to get a timetable down on paper. D-M might really have a good idea here. As I said, there are a few things which will need watching. I can think of some customers, for instance, who wouldn't be impressed by having somebody from behind a turret lathe sitting in their office. But that sort of thing is a detail and we'll work it out; the idea itself is so good that we simply have to do it.

And if I get any headwind from any of my people about having a co-pilot flying with them, I'll light a fire under them which will burn their arses to a crisp.

April

27 Friday

What am I do to about Ken Milburn? At 10.30 this morning he turned up in my office and said, 'Can I talk to you, please, Tom?'

It was on the tip of my tongue to say, 'What the hell are you doing out of your territory in the middle of the morning?' but one look at him shut my mouth. Compared to his countenance Dox Quixote's would have looked overjoyed. I said, 'Sit down, Ken. What is it?'

Damn me if his eyes didn't start filling with tears again. I thought, oh God, no. Not his idiot wife – what was her name? Joanne? – again.

It *was* his wife. He said, 'Tom, I'm so sorry to bother you but I haven't anybody else to talk to. Joanne says now that she won't leave me, she'll stay, but she won't – she won't – '

'She won't what, Ken?' I don't get *paid* enough for this.

'She won't. She says, no sex. She won't let me – ' He put his face in his hands. He said through his fingers, 'Tom, won't you talk to her?'

I felt that I was losing touch with reality. There is no chapter on this sort of thing in the management books. I could just see myself saying to Joanne, 'Look, sunshine, this "No sex, please, we're British" idea of yours has got one of my salesmen dropping down the sales chart. Come on, let him have a little cuddle now and then or he'll be selling shoelaces on the corner, because I shall have to fire him.' Sorry as I was for Ken I felt an insane desire to burst out laughing. As I remembered, his Joanne had a sort of 34-34-34 figure, and it wasn't easy picturing her as an object of desire. Looking at Ken's miserable face I became ashamed of myself. He was suffering, and it must have taken courage to come and see me and to bare his soul.

I said, 'Ken, I can't do it. Joanne wouldn't stand for my intruding

on something as deeply personal as . . . as your intimate relations.'
He was about to start all over again. I said desperately, 'Look, there
are specialists who can handle this sort of thing. Let me find out more
about it and I'll get back to you. All right?' Ken looked doubtful, but
at last he nodded, and I got him out of the office somehow.

I called Dorcas in and said, '*Are* there such things as marriage
counsellors, or do they exist only in Andy Capp?'

She said, 'Poor Mr Milburn; still with problems? I will find.'

She found the name of some centre – I don't know where she got it
and I don't want to know – and gave it to me. I have it on my desk,
and now what do I do with it? I can't very well call Ken at home and
give it to him and I don't want to put it in his pigeon-hole at work. I'll
get it to him somehow.

An up-and-down sort of week; and my beloved white-haired
mother wonders what I do all day, 'Sitting behind that big desk,
dear.'

April

30 Monday

Sat down with Mac and hammered out a timetable for his people to go out with mine. Not as easy as it seemed to be when D-M first produced the idea. I can only use my Central salesmen, of course; we can't have factory staff rushing around Northumberland and staying away from home for two or three nights. Salesmen's families are used to that sort of treatment, but I don't think a machinist's wife would be very impressed by it.

Then, as I told Mac, there are customers who simply will not permit more than one person at a time to call on them. Busy supermarkets, for instance, will not allow a deputation into their places of business, and if you want to keep their goodwill and their business, you honour their feelings about this. We have one or two places where I can't even go in with my own salesman. Mac said, 'That doesn't much matter, Tom. I don't mind if they have to stay outside on some of the calls. It's the whole thing of getting into a car, going out on calls, being introduced to the customer, listening to the salesman giving his presentation – and to the customer raising objections and showing resistance.'

'And complaining like hell because Dispatch didn't send the right stuff,' I said.

Mac said, 'Exactly, lad. That's the sort of thing which will do some good.' He looked at me sharply. 'Are you for this idea, Tom? You don't feel that you have been pushed into it by Dunsby-Martin?'

Mac is nobody's fool. I was for it in principle, sure; it was just that I wasn't completely certain that there weren't some aspects of it that would blow up in my face. I have customers out there who are very valuable to me in terms of sales volume and whom I would hate to lose. What if a journeyman just happened to say the wrong thing at

81

the wrong time? I said with emphasis, 'Heavens no, Mac! I'm all for it. Great idea.'

He said, 'You needn't worry that my boys will let the side down. They will be neatly dressed for the occasion.' He smiled to show that he was gently pulling my leg.

I said, 'Hey, come off it, Mac. Your people will probably be better dressed than my bunch of tearaways. I'm not worried.'

Well, we shall see. The scheme starts today week and I am meeting with my Central team on Friday to tell them about it. Can't wait to see what their reaction will be. Approval? Grudging acceptance? Dismay? Mutiny?

What an exciting job I've got.

May

4 Friday

Had the meeting with the Central boys and told them that from next week they are going to have navigators sitting next to them for two days a week until further notice.

Interesting reaction, or set of reactions. Some said, 'Fine, good idea.' A couple had no reaction at all, but those particular two would have no reaction if I told them that their territories had been expanded to include the north face of the Eiger. Two had negative reactions, each for his own reasons. Guy Bishop said, 'What? Have some clown hanging around my neck? Damn it, Tom, I work alone; you know that.'

'I said, 'He won't be a co-worker. He is purely an observer. You introduce him and then carry on as if he wasn't there.' Bishop looked black, but he subsided.

The second complainer was Gregory Foy, and I know exactly what *his* problem is. I have been keeping a beady eye on Greg recently because I am sure he is dragging his feet. Now, if that's true then the last thing he would want would be a spectator to witness his laziness. All right, chum; maybe this is a very good way to see if your performance improves when someone is out there with you, and if it does you will have some explaining to do.

I gave them the home telephone numbers of the people they will be taking out and told them to arrange pick-up times and places.

May

8 Tuesday

Wendy Carlton and Brian Hook have now been through their internal training, having spent the past two weeks on the order telephones. I always think that no salesperson should ever go out on the road without having spent some time in the Order Department, taking orders on the phone and handling those that the sales force bring in or send in. This teaches them the absolute necessity of getting an order down on paper legibly, accurately and fully when they go out and start writing orders themselves, and it saves God knows how much time, effort and money for the company.

Anyway, they are now ready to be blooded in the field, and today, the day after the bank holiday, I took Wendy out to see some customers. We spent the morning making calls and over a burger at a steakhouse I asked, 'How do you feel after half a day in the field?'

She said, 'Fine! I've enjoyed it very much.'

'Anything about the morning impress you in any way?'

She smiled. 'I was just thinking what a nice lot of people our customers seem to be.'

'Why "nice"?'

She said, 'Well, they were all so pleasant and friendly. Why, we even got offered tea three times in one morning!'

I said, 'Yes, but did you notice another thing about this morning?'

'What was that?'

'We didn't get a single order.'

She made a face. 'I did notice, and I was going to ask you about that. Was it because of the *sort* of customers we called on?'

'Good for you. Yes, we were calling on customers who buy from us either on a contract, which means that we have made moulds for them and they are tied to us for two or three years, or buy on imprest.'

'Imprest?' This was a new one on her.

'Imprest. The dictionary says it means "an advance from government funds". In our business it means that a company keeps a steady stock of, say, ten cases of half-pint sun-tan lotion bottles. At the end of each fortnight our sales person checks their stock. If they are down to four cases, our sales person automatically writes an order for six cases to bring them back to the agreed stock figure.'

She said, 'Oh. Order-taking, in fact. Not creative selling.' She sounded disappointed.

I said, 'Hey, Wendy – don't knock order-taking. I would love to have my whole sales force rushing around all day taking orders. But when you say that contract or imprest selling is merely writing up the order, don't forget that in the beginning, to get these people to become our customers, a hell of a good piece of creative selling was done. The sales person who toddles in, counts the cases on the shelves and rocks out with a fat order, probably called on that company for weeks or even months before they made the final presentation which netted the contract. They may be gathering in the sheaves now, but they worked their arses off to plant the seed.' I caught myself. 'Sorry; let's say they worked hard.'

Wendy emptied her glass of milk and sat back. 'Tom, let's talk. This had to come up sooner or later. I'm well aware that I am the only woman in a team of men. Now, I need to be accepted by my male colleagues, and I won't be if they are all worrying about their language in front of me. Okay?'

I said doubtfully, 'I see your point, but I think that the men on the team are naturally going to be a little careful with the four-letter words.'

She said earnestly, 'Well, they'll have to get over it, and you can help, Tom, by not treating me any differently from anyone else.'

I could see that this meant a lot to her. 'All right, Wendy; I'll try, and I expect that when they get used to you the boys will stop thinking of you as a Vestal Virgin.'

'Thank you for taking me seriously on this.'

'Wendy, you are one of my team. Anything that is serious and important to you is serious and important to me.'

She looked relieved. 'I'm so pleased that we can talk freely; I think that's so important in a relationship with a manager.'

I said, 'Well, thanks; that's a compliment. I hope you will always feel that you can talk to me about anything that bugs you – anything at all.' I thought of Ken Milburn and I was tempted to say, 'Almost anything, that is. Just don't bring your personal problems to me.' I didn't say it because I'd just had a glimpse of this lady's inner core of toughness and I couldn't see her coming in to cry on my shoulder. I reached for the bill and said, 'In the meantime let's get back to work or my boss will be using some four-letter words about our sales figures.'

Wendy said, 'Halvies on the bill.'

'No. I appreciate equal rights and all that, but when I go out with any member of my team the lunch is on my expense account.'

She said, 'Is that true? You wouldn't bullshit me?' I stared at her. She grinned. 'Sorry, Tom; that slipped out. Let's say, you wouldn't kid me?'

I said, 'Hey, you don't have to moderate your language on my account. I was the only boy in a family of four, and my sisters taught me all the four- and eight-letter words early in life.'

She laughed. 'I think you're right. It *will* work out.'

I said, 'I'm sure it will. However, this afternoon we will be calling on some really tough sons of guns.' Wendy opened her mouth. I said, 'Let's leave at at "guns". You will see the darker side of some of our customers. Just keep your mouth closed and your ears open and don't get upset if the call begins to sound nasty. These are customers who believe that they have a real grievance against the company, and sometimes it's best for the Sales Manager to handle these himself, because the problem may be above the sales person's level of authority to handle. The thing to remember is that when they start shouting, there's nothing *personal* about it. They are not yelling at you, although it looks as though they hate you. You are the receptacle for their bile and bad temper, that's all. Actually, you may learn some brand-new words which even *you* didn't know!'

She said, 'Exciting! Lead me to them.'

I may have a good one here.

May

9 Wednesday

Spent the day with Brian Hook, and I wonder if I have a problem here? Perhaps it's too soon to tell. The thing is that Brian came across so well in the interviews, and his report from the recruitment agency was so positive that perhaps I was expecting too much.

Why am I disappointed? Well, first, I tend to judge salespeoples' attitudes, intelligence and suitability for the job by the questions they ask when I take them out into the field for the first time. It is all so new that there must be many things which they need to ask, and I make it clear in the beginning that anything they don't understand they just ask about. Now yesterday Wendy's questions were perceptive and to the point. Today Brian hardly had a single question. To every piece of information I gave him he said, 'Is that so?' Until I could have screamed.

The worst thing was that by about 3.00 pm, he actually began yawning – he was bored, damn it! All right, I was doing all the talking on the calls and he was just a bystander, but everything he was seeing and hearing should have been interesting, and it obviously wasn't. And this was his career we were concerned with out there, not a trip on a sightseeing bus.

Well, perhaps it is early days yet. He may be one of those sales people who get bored going around as second fiddle and only open up when they are flying solo.

I hope so. I picked Brian and I hope he doesn't turn out to be a non-doer. A manager is judged by his team and Brian wasn't one of the old boys wished on me by Bert Corley, he is *my* man.

MEMO TO ME: Stay as close to Brian as pips on a strawberry. One sign of substandard work and leap to the rescue.

May

16 Wednesday

D-M walked in and dropped a leaflet on my dessk. The headline read, 'Finance For Non-financial People', and it was a course of some sort. I flipped through it and looked at D-M.

He said, 'Why not go on that?'

'Me? I'm a salesman. I leave that money stuff to Don, and he's welcome to it.'

D-M was patient. 'Managers of any sort – Sales, Production, Personnel – should know the basics of business accounting. You should be able to listen to Don and understand what he is talking about. One day it might be very useful to you.'

I'm not dim: paint it in fifty-foot letters on the side of a balloon and fly it outside my window and sooner or later I'll get the message. I said, 'Fine idea, D-M. I'll get on to these people right away. Looking forward to it.' He looked at me for a moment, nodded, and drifted out.

Over dinner I told Annabel that I was going on an accounting course. She snorted delicately. 'You? You *hate* money matters. Who has to balance your cheque-book? Me!'

'That's just the point. If I am ever to become a Director of Hutton Horner, I have to be able to understand P and L and trial balances and – oh, things like that. The thing is that D-M hinted more or less the same thing when he told me about the course.' I said, 'It's a bit of a nuisance, three evenings a week for two months. On the other hand it will be worth it to – '

Annabel wasn't listening. She said dreamily, 'My husband, the Director,' and got up and poured us two liqueurs.

Thomas Liskeard, Sales Director. Look me over, boys.

May

18 Friday

The last entry in my diary was a big swank about 'Thomas Liskeard, Sales Director'. That was two days ago. If I make another booboo like the one which surfaced today, it will be 'Tom Liskeard, ex-sales Manager, now unemployed'.

As I said, the booboo surfaced today. I didn't conceive it today, that was some months ago; today was the day it rose up and bit me in the jugular. What happened was this. Our financial year starts on 1 February, and our sales team always gets off to a sluggish start. This is because they have usually been working flat out getting as much sales volume as possible before the end of January, to make the final figures for last year as good as possible. Having done this they feel that they don't owe the company one old penny, and they all tend to go on a sort of work-to-rule slow-down.

Now this means that the figures for February and March are usually poor, and *that* means that we have to battle to regain lost ground for three or four months after that. It's like trying to keep up a sixty-mile-an-hour average on a long trip; if you slow down for five minutes it takes ages before you make up the lost time and you have to go like mad to do it.

So Liskeard has the brilliant idea of having an incentive scheme for the first three months of the new financial year. Every person who reaches quota for the month qualifies for bonus points, the further over their quota, the more points gained. So many points, so much lolly in the sales person's back pocket. Points to work on a sliding scale, so that a really good month could mean a lot of lolly.

Great idea, and fully approved of by D-M. I also pulled Don Thorpe in because I didn't want him to say later that I had been wasting the company's money. He looked over the details with a sour face – he hates giving sales people money, thinks they earn too much already – and he admitted that he couldn't see anything wrong with it.

Well, there *was* something wrong with it and, while perhaps Don or D-M should have picked it up, I was the one who thought of it in the first place and I was the one who blew it.

What is that old saying? 'A salesman is someone who gives his efforts to the company and his talents to his expense account.' When will I learn that the moment you tell a salesman about a change of some sort in their territory, salary, car plan or retirement fund, he starts looking for a loophole, and if there is the slightest little chink he will find it?

The problem was with the sliding-scale idea. On paper it makes a lot of sense; usually when a salesman reaches target for the month, with perhaps a little bit over as insurance against cancelled orders, he will tend to go into neutral and coast for a while. The sliding scale, which gave more cash per unit sold the higher he went, was supposed to circumvent this.

It circumvented it, all right. What those cunning sods have been doing – most of them, anyway – was to get their quotas in February and March, and to just reach them, nothing more. I had been watching the figures during the course of the scheme and I had noticed that most of the team had not done outstandingly well for the first two months; that most had only just reached quota. (Did I say that a salesman had to *make* quota every month in order to qualify for the scheme? A built-in fail-safe, or so I thought.)

Now the returns have come in for April, the final month of the scheme, and while I should be delighted at the figures because they are through the roof, the problem is that Don Thorpe is also through the roof. My clever sales team, or most of them, have cunningly nursed their customers along for February and March, and the moment that the first day of April dawned they went in there like a swarm of locusts and hit everyone for orders as hard as they could. So the sliding scale has worked beautifully for them, we are faced with a big pay-out, and I am left looking like a twit. Which I am for not seeing the loop-hole in the scheme.

Of course, as soon as he saw the figures, Don Thorpe ran crying to mummy. D-M called me into his office and there was cry-baby Thorpe with the evidence all spread out over D-M's desk. D-M said, 'Tom, Don has just shown me the returns for the incentive plan. It seems that we blundered somehow.' Translation: 'Your incentive plan. You blundered. Somehow.'

I said, 'Yes, D-M. I thought that the sliding scale would be good motivation for the men to get out and sell, and I was sure that I'd covered myself with the qualifying rule. I was wrong, and it has cost us a lot more than I thought it would. I simply didn't think it through.' One of the best ways to stop people from telling you that you have been an idiot is to tell *them* that you have been an idiot. At least it spiked Thorpe's guns.

D-M said, 'Yes. Well, there's nothing we can do about it now.'

Then Don stuck his nose in. He said, talking very obviously to D-M and ignoring me, 'I think that we have a good case for reducing the amount of the cash awards. We can simply tell the sales staff that an error was made,' he flicked a glance at me, 'in calculating the percentages, and that the awards will be reduced by thirty per cent. That will still give them adequate return for whatever efforts they may have made.'

Trust a bloody accountant. I was just about to blast him when D-M, who must have seen the expression on my face, intervened. 'No, Don, we are committed to the awards as they stand; we can't go back on our word. The sales force has earned the money – not without some guile, but with no real malice – and we must pay out. We can't at this stage . . . What is that colourful phrase that is going around?' He looked at me.

I muttered, 'Move the goalposts.' I was still boiling.

'Ah, yes. From across the Atlantic, I gather. We can't move the goalposts to suit ourselves.' He looked at me. 'Well, we have learnt something from this affair.' Translation: 'Let's hope that you have learnt something from this balls-up of yours.'

I said, '*I* certainly have.' Might as well throw myself on the mercy of the court. Don Thorpe gathered his papers together, looking like the cat who has found the cream jug unguarded. I got up, prepared to go out and throw a rope over a beam.

D-M wasn't quite finished. He said, 'However, let's not forget one thing.' He smiled gently at me. 'Your men, no matter under what compulsion, did after all bring the sales in, which was the object of the exercise. It was the best April ever, was it not?'

All my sulks gone, I said, 'Yes. It was. Thank you, D-M.'

So I got out of the business with my skin intact and no blood shed, and at the expense of a slightly scratched ego.

MEMO TO ME: When you make any change in your sales force's circumstances, *think as they do*. You once trod where they now tread – it shouldn't be too difficult.

May

22 Tuesday

Annabel dropped Pete into the office today while she went shopping with Angie. My daughter is growing fast and apparently needs a whole new wardrobe. She loves being fitted out with clothes and is very good in shops, while you practically have to shoot Pete with a tranquilising dart to get him through the door.

Pete is no trouble in the office and since he told me, in the strictest confidence, that he intends to marry Dorcas when he grows up, the two of them get along pretty well. He sharpens her pencils in the machine and he even knows how to switch on the word-processor and write his name on it.

Mac dropped into the office and was introduced to Pete. He said, 'Are you going to be a Sales Manager like your father, laddie?' Pete said, 'No, I'm going to Mauritius to protect animals' – this was the result of seeing a Gerald Durrell feature on television last week. When Pete and Dorcas had brought us coffee, Mac said, 'How would you feel if he decided to be a salesman, Tom?'

Ask most fathers, no matter how they earn their living, if they want their sons to follow in their footsteps and their answer would be, 'My god, no! I wouldn't wish this job on my worst enemy.' They say this whether they mean it or not, it's simply something which fathers are supposed to say. I had never really thought about it. I said, 'Why not? The selling business is a good way to climb up the promotion ladder in a company. Pete is already a "people" person, and he likes talking. Who knows, he might be good at it.' I thought a moment and said, 'Only thing is, I'd want him to go to university first and get a degree of some sort. I have a feeling that my generation is the last one that could get away with walking into a good job without any qualifications.'

Mac said, 'What subjects would you want him to take?' I looked at him in surprise; Mac doesn't usually indulge in chit-chat.

'It's not just idle curiosity, Tom. I've a lad at home, rising sixteen now, and he's not interested in engineering so he won't be following me into the profession. I thought he might be interested in selling.'

I said, 'Well, Mac, there are so many things he could do these days. I suppose a BA, majoring in Psychology, wouldn't do him any harm, or, of course, Marketing.'

'Can you get a degree in Marketing itself?'

'You can indeed,' I said. 'I'd like to have the letters behind my own name.'

Talking to Mac made me realise that I must sometime get some information on part-time courses, and get D-M's okay on offering them to my sales people. The usual thing is that the company pays for the course, the salesman pays the company back on the never-never, and if and when the salesman passes and gets his diploma the company refunds what he has paid, so that he gets the training for nothing. It's not as philanthropic as it sounds. Firstly, the costs are tax-deductible for the company, and secondly, it's a very good way of keeping good people with you. A person is not so likely to leave if he is are halfway through a course which will cost him nothing if he passes and is still with us.

What Mac had come for was to give me his first impressions of the reactions to his people going out with my sales force; what my lot were apparently calling Liskeard's Taxi Company. So far, he was reasonably pleased. Of the eleven who had been out, six had been enthusiastic, three had shown no marked feeling either for or against, and two had disliked it and did not want to go again. I asked for the names of the last two and made a note to check on it; their negative reaction could have been from the negative attitude of the salesmen who took them out. I'll follow it up and see how they feel and if they didn't like it I'll take them off the rota. I said, 'How do you feel, Mac? Do you think we should carry on with it?'

'Certainly I do,' said Mac. 'I have to be careful that I don't strip my production lines of key people when there's a rush, but I think it is doing some good.' He smiled. 'D'you know, Tom, one of my lads came to me yesterday after spending a day in the field, and he said, "Mr MacLeod, those salesmen meet some very rude people, and they can't answer back!"'

I said, 'Well, now; fancy that.'

'And another one told Ron Aston, "Hell, it's not easy just finding parking for the car twelve times a day!"'

So we must be doing something right. We agreed to carry on for the meantime and not report back to D-M until we had more reactions, both from the factory people as well as the sales force.

Writing this, another idea has struck me, and I think this one also makes sense. It's a sort of spin-off from D-M's idea of factory people going out with sales people. Why not take my sales people out of the field for two or three days at a time and give them to Jimmy Liss, the Chief Order Clerk? Jimmy would love to have them, and it would do some of them a world of good to have their ears glued to an order telephone. When Wendy and Brian went through basic training I decided to have them join the Order Department for a while, but the older sales staff have never been through that, and it is high time they did. Incorrectly filled-in orders are the bane of Jimmy's life, and they can end up making the Sales Division look stupid.

For example: A month ago Ted Formby phoned me from Birmingham, as mad as a snake because an important order for one of his biggest customers hadn't even been processed, three days before he had promised that it would be delivered. Irritated, I told Dicky Bird to drop everything and track it down. It took him two hours – he eventually found it in Ron Aston's HOLD file. When Dicky reported this to me and I started shouting the odds to Ron, he simply showed me the order, written and signed by Ted Formby. In the slots for COLOUR and WIDTH Ted had scribbled 'TBA' ('to be advised'). Ron said, 'Tom, he *hasn't* advised us; not a word. Now, shall we make it in pink and two inches wide, or purple and five feet wide?'

I apologised to Ron who is a busy man, went back to the office and wrote a letter to Ted Formby which had Dorcas saying, 'When the poor man reads this he is cutting his throat, I can tell you.'

MEMO TO ME: Get together with Jimmy Liss. If he agrees, let's do this without telling D-M. Tell him when it is already a success. Why should I ask him which leg to put in my pants first?

May

25 Friday

Beginning to get things moving for the conference. The venue is fixed – a stately home type of place outside Dublin. The sales staff have been told well in advance; I don't want anyone saying that they can't make it because it clashes with their grandparents' diamond wedding anniversary or elective surgery on a varicose vein. Everybody seems to be excited about Ireland – obviously one of D-M's better ideas.

However, it is absolutely *impossible* to foresee all the problems. Had I sat down and thought for a week I wouldn't have come up with the snag that hit my desk this afternoon. I received a letter from Eddie Blawith, my man in Ipswich. Very apologetic: he would love to go to Ireland for the conference but he can't fly. Very sorry, but there it is and he hopes that I will understand.

'Can't fly? What the hell does he mean, he can't fly?'

Dorcas said, 'He means that he has a – in French, it is *effroi*. Terror; no, not a terror – '

'Phobia?'

'Thank you. Phobia. He has a phobia about flying. Many people have it.'

'But heavens, a short trip like this?'

Dorcas said, 'Tom. I had a cousin. In Hungary in 1956 he jumped on top of a Russian tank, stabbed the officer dead and threw a grenade into the turret, and he was only sixteen years old.'

'A very brave boy.'

She nodded. 'Very brave. But he could not climb into an aircraft to save his life. Your Mr Blawith could be so brave he could earn the James Cross – '

'George Cross.'

'Thank you. George Cross. But he cannot fly. *Bien*. We put him on a boat. He steams over, we fly over, everyone is happy.'

I said, 'Write and tell him that he steams over and no doubt he will be happy.'

She produced a letter from the folder on her lap. 'Is already written. Please to sign.'

I'm taking Dorcas to Ireland, of course. I don't think I could contemplate running this conference without her. I have a feeling that she will get on with the Irish like blood-brothers.

Talking to D-M about the conference and exactly who should attend, I said, 'What about Michelle Sherborne?' Now, what on earth made me come out with that? D-M thought for a moment and said, 'Good idea. She will do her job much more effectively if she knows what is going on in Sales. I have had the thought that you and she should have more contact with each other.'

I looked at him, but there was nothing behind the words. I left his office scratching my head. Actually, it did make sense for the PRO of the company to be involved in Sales because, although most PROs recoil in distaste if you mention it, the end result of good public relations is more sales for the company.

But was that really why I had suggested that Michelle be one of the party? Or was my subconscious licking its lips at having her around for three days and, God help us, nights, far away from hearth and home?

'Nah!' I said, to the surprise of Ellen the tea-lady, as she pushed her trolley past me in the passage.

May

30 Wednesday

I can't go far in any direction these days without bumping into something to do with the sales conference. I had done a good job sorting out the sleeping arrangements in the conference venue (suite for D-M, singles for management, doubling up for the sales people – rank still has its privileges) and had passed my rough notes on to Dorcas for typing and putting in the conference packages.

She walked back into my office and gave the sheet back to me. She said, 'I know that you are worried about Mr Milburn's personal problems, but I do not think that his wife would approve of this arrangement.'

'What?' Then I looked at what I had written. Neatly bracketed together in one room I had put Milburn, K.A. and Carlton, W. 'Oh lord. As you say, Dorcas, I'd like to help Ken, but this is a sales conference, not a sex therapy session. Also, I don't think that Wendy would be all that impressed.' I changed the list to give Wendy a room to herself and put Ken in with the odd man. Lucky we had an odd number of sales people. 'Bloody odd, come to think of it,' I muttered as I gave the sheet back to Dorcas.

'I beg your forgiveness?'

'Pardon,' I corrected. Amazing how Dorcas can get through a long and complex sentence without a flaw and then fall down on a simple word. Equally amazing that it doesn't happen in her letters, only her speech.

'Thank you. Pardon?'

'It was nothing, Dorcas. I just wonder sometimes why I haven't got a *normal* sales team.'

Dorcas sniffed. 'You are saying in one of your letters that the tone of a working group is determined by the person in charge of that group.'

'Go to hell, Dorcas.'

'Not now. Now I make coffee.'

I have been sitting with the diary on my lap after writing that last bit and I must have been staring at nothing because Annabel switched off the weather forecast and said, 'Many meteorites out there tonight?'

I said, 'Was I staring into space? I was thinking about the conference.'

'Surprise, surprise. These days you think about nothing else but that silly conference.'

'Sorry. Am I not giving you and Pete and Angie enough time?'

Annabel smiled. 'You give us enough time, and I'm not complaining, and it isn't a silly conference. I know how important it is that it goes off well. It's just . . . what's the special problem tonight?' Now, it is generous of Annabel to ask a question like that because anything to do with business bores her stiff. Even so, I have had some good ideas by airing problems with her as she sits knitting or sewing or making dolls and bears for the children.

I said, 'Let me strip the bark off this one for you and see if the sap flows.'

'Thomas!' Annabel hates buzz-words even more than D-M does.

'Sorry. The thing is, there will be two sessions in the conference devoted to product knowledge. Mac McLeod is going to do one of them from the technical point of view and I'll be doing the other from the sales angle. Now in that room there will be some of the real old guard – salesmen who have been there for fifteen years and more. There will also be much less experienced people, right up to the brand-new ones like Wendy Carlton and Brian Hook.'

'So?'

'So how do I handle the different attitudes in that room? On the onc hand I have the newer ones and I can't run it at too sophisticated a level because I'll only bewilder them and make them depressed and worried. On the other hand there are the tough old buggers whose "best before this date" has long expired and who think they know everything.'

'Do they know everything?' Annabel has a way of getting to the heart of the matter.

'No, they damn well don't and they can all do with some basic product training, but if I try to give it to them I can see them sit back, look sideways at each other, and just switch off.' I paused. 'There's another thing that makes it even tougher. Remember that I have been with HH for less than five years and I am now the Sales Manager. Some of those diehards have been there for three times longer than I have and some of them are ten or twelve years older than me. How do I get them to start at page one of the product manuals and plough through them for the umpteenth time?'

Annabel waved her glass at me and I gave each of us a refill. She said, 'Do you remember when we went to the charity première of *Swan Lake?*'

I said, 'Do I not. Cost me a fortune to see a lot of people rushing around a stage proving all over again that what goes up must come down.'

'Barbarian. Do you remember the prima ballerina?'

'The boss lady of the Swans.'

'Well,' Annabel said, 'that "boss lady", as you call her, is world famous. She has danced that rôle of Odette Odile all over the world and it practically belongs to her. She is one of the immortals of ballet.'

'I take it this has something to do with my sales conference and that you will be explaining the connection sooner or later.'

Annabel said composedly, 'Be quiet. Now, the morning after that performance there would have been a practice session for the whole *corps de ballet*. Everyone has to be there, no exceptions. They all work at the *barre*. They all have to practise basic steps – *entrechat, plié, arabesque, jeté,* and so on.'

'Good for them. What about it?'

'Didn't you listen? They *all* go through it. The prime ballerina, the male lead – *everyone*. No matter if they are world renowned or the newest member of the corps, they all turn up the next morning and go through the basics, and the "boss lady" gets hell from the ballet master if her hand position isn't right, just as the novice does.'

I said, 'Is that true? Everyone has to do the basics?'

'No exceptions.'

I went over and kissed the top of her head. 'You have just given me my introduction to the product training session. You are clever. Thank you.'

'You're welcome. Now that you are no longer worrying about your conference, perhaps we can talk about something *really* important. Do you think that Angie should have recorder lessons?'

June

4 Monday

I am trying to do something which may be impossible. Is there any way to measure a person's motivation? To quantify it, if you like what Dorcas calls hum-words? I have been fooling around with a sort of chart – a bar graph. Easy enough to do: just take a piece of paper and draw a horizontal line through its middle. At the top of the page put PLUS 100, at the bottom put MINUS 100. The line itself is ZERO.

Now, nobody would ever get a PLUS 100, because he would be able to leap tall buildings with a single bound and fly faster than a speeding bullet. Equally, nobody would be MINUS 100 because he would immediately cut his throat. Everybody is somewhere on the chart: the angels on my sales team are up there, well above the line; the problem children are down below.

Have I invented something worthwhile here, or am I wasting my time and the company's graph paper? Today I tried to chart a couple of examples, and the first one was my ever-present problem Ken Milburn. I drew a bar below the ZERO line, reaching to MINUS 30. Last week it would have been worse, say, MINUS 50, but he seems to be trying to stagger to his feet and rejoin the human race; his figures have taken a slight upward turn. I am not going to ask him the reason for the improvement; I do not need in my innocent young life a graphic description of what is going on behind the Milburns' bedroom door. He is not up to standard, nothing like it, but at least he is not getting worse.

Then I took David Lundy, my Welsh salesman. I put his bar above the line, about PLUS 25. When I had done this I got interested. Why had I not given David a higher rating? He's a good man, steady and reliable, and his figures are usually quite satisfactory. There must, I thought, be something in the back of my mind. It

100

made me think of the last time I went to Wales and spent some time with David. I got Dorcas to pull out my field appraisals of him, and there it was. I had, I saw, given him fairly good ratings for most of the sections but my remark at the bottom of the last form was: 'Doesn't seem to feel that he has to try too hard. Skimming the cream off a high-potential territory.'

This can happen, of course, especially where a salesman is situated a fair distance from head office, so that his manager doesn't see him as often as he does a man nearer home base. He can find himself in a territory where the pickings are not rich enough to warrant two salesmen but are enough to make it no sweat for one man to produce good-looking figures.

I remembered that I'd felt that David could have exerted himself just a little bit more. This made me, when I had to put him on my bar graph, rate him lower than I otherwise would have.

Setting this motivation graph of mine aside for the moment, let me think about Wales. It isn't David Lundy's fault that Wales is too big for one man and not big enough, in terms of potential, for two, but it does mean that we are losing business which could be ours because one man can't service all the potential customers. Yet I can't very well expand the territory of one of the Birmingham men, for instance, and give him part of North Wales; he'd go mad rushing back and forth, and the type of business he would have to handle would be so different from the highly industrialised Midlands – impossible.

I shall have to watch the potential there and, eventually, put in another man. This will make David Lundy scream in agony, because his easy life will change dramatically to where he will have to scratch for every penny he brings in. And I will have the delightful job of calculating new quotas for the two territories. Hooray.

June

6 Wednesday

Michelle Sherborne called me, very excited. D-M has told her that she is coming on the sales conference. She is sure that I must have suggested it and thank you, thank you, thank you! Why me? Then I remember – my God, yes – I did mention her name to D-M.

What she wanted was to come and see me to discuss her part in the conference. What part? All she will have to do is sit there and keep her mouth shut, and I almost told her so. No, from what I was hearing on the phone, D-M has had another of his brilliant ideas and thinks that it would be a good thing if the sales force knew more about Public Relations. So he has told Michelle to see me and ask me if I can squeeze her into the agenda for thirty minutes to give a talk on PR.

I thought about it and it made sense. My people know nothing about PR and care less, and perhaps they should be exposed to it, however briefly.

I said, 'Fine, Michelle. Sure, we can fit you in.'

'Marvellous! Tom, may I come and see you about it? What about Friday afternoon at 4.30? *Our* time.'

Oh, boy. Already 4.30 was *our* time. I muttered an, 'Okay, see you then.' I stuck my head into the outer office and said, 'Michelle Sherborne, 4.30 Friday.' Dorcas made a note on my calendar and turned to look at me cynically. I stuck my tongue out at her and went back to my desk.

'*Our* time.' Good God.

June

7 Thursday

Damn me if Ken Milburn didn't come in again. He turned up at lunchtime so I couldn't blast him for wasting selling time; he was only wasting my lunch hour which is always interrupted somehow or other, even though Dorcas does her best to keep calls and callers away from me between one and two. 'You need your rest from your being in labour.'

'From my labours.'

'Thank you. From your labours. But it is Mr Milburn, and perhaps he is a special case?'

'Yes, I suppose so. Show him in.' I steeled myself for another emotional episode in the saga of Ken's domestic life.

But it was a different Ken Milburn who barged in and pumped my hand. He wasn't very coherent, but the gist of his outpourings was that he and Joanne had gone to the centre and had joined a group therapy class and had both bared their souls and found themselves, and anyway their marriage was fine and everything in the garden was rosy. I congratulated him and finally retrieved my hand. I said, 'Fine, Ken. No more problems, then?'

Which, as it turned out, was the wrong thing to say. His face fell: yes, as it happened there was still a problem. He blushed and stuttered and hesitated until I said, 'Ken, what are you trying to say?'

What he was trying to say was that now that everything in the marriage was fine, Joanne hated him to go away on a trip even for a single night. His eyes had shifted away when he had said that *every-thing* was fine, and I got the message. Staring intently at my Garfield paperweight he said, 'Joanne was wondering if you – well, she said I should ask you if you could change my territory so that I wouldn't have to make any trips which would keep me away over . . . overnight.'

103

I stared at him. I was getting more than a little pissed off with Ken and his problems. 'Ken, you spend, what is it, four nights a month away from home. There are colleagues of yours who sleep away from their families one night in three. Tell your wife that you and she are very lucky, and that I do not intend to move my sales force around to suit you.'

I thought that should cover it, but Ken showed no sign of leaving. He looked stubborn, which was a new look for him. He said, 'Tom, I don't like to say this because you have been very good to me, but if you can't see your way clear to changing my territory, I'll have to . . .' He gulped. 'I'll have to . . .' He was having trouble getting the cork out.

I helped him out. 'You are saying that either I change your territory so that you can stay at home every night, or you will leave the company, is that right?' Ken nodded, still studying Garfield.

I sat back and scrubbed my face with my hands. 'Ken, my first reaction is to tell you to get out of here, surrender your manuals, park your car in the yard and leave. You have just given me an ultimatum, and if you think I'm going to submit to that, then not only do you not know much about how companies are run, you also don't know me.' Ken's mouth fell open. I don't know what he expected from me but it obviously wasn't this. I went on. 'I am not shifting you. There are only two salesmen with territories where they don't spend nights away from home, and both of those territories are too important to trust to you.' I was controlling myself with difficulty. 'I'm not shifting you, but I'm also not accepting your resignation. I want you to go away and think very carefully about the job you have here in Hutton Horner. Talk it over with your wife. Think about the sort of job you could get in selling if you applied to any sales company with the condition that you never spend a night away from home.'

Ken said, 'Oh!' Great balls of fire, he hadn't even thought about that.

I said, 'I want you back in this office this time next week and I shall want from you either your written resignation or your promise that from now on you will keep your personal problems out of your working life, and put your mind totally to doing better than you have been doing. That's all.' He shot out of the office like a startled rabbit.

Dorcas looked in. 'Mr Milburn was leaving like Alain Prost. You threaten him with violent death, perhaps?'

'Not exactly.' I told her that the centre she had found for the Milburns had worked so well that the lovebirds no longer wanted to be separated for a single night.

'Goodness gracious. With Mrs Milburn it is like that old Mr Sinatra song: "All, or nothing at all".'

When she had left, I got up from my desk and walked over to the window. Ken's Vauxhall was pulling out of the car park and it seemed that it was moving faster than it usually did.

Had I been too tough with him? On the question of his ultimatum (ultimatum as in attempted blackmail), no; I had handled that properly. Many managers would have fired Ken on the turn, without giving him a chance to recant. You simply can't let anyone get away with that.

There was one thing I wasn't very proud of, though. I had said, 'Both of those territories are too important to trust to you.' Thinking back on that I had a sour taste in my mouth. What had my first manager once said to me? 'Tom, when you are in a management position you will have occasion to reprimand your people. Two rules: One, *never* do it in public. Come down on them as hard as you like, but do it behind a closed door.' Well, that was all right, I had done that. But he had also said, 'Two, give them seven sorts of hell by all means, but don't say anything to impair their self-respect. Man is an odd creature; you can rob him blind, burn his house down, even try to kill him, and he will still make excuses for you and forgive you. But tarnish his image of himself, and you destroy him, and he will hate you as long as he lives.'

This morning with Ken Milburn I did the unforgiveable thing; I had hurt his self-esteem, and sitting here now I realise that I would give a lot to be able to take those words back. Trouble was that I had let myself become intensely annoyed with Ken on a *personal* level, and I threw that remark at him *intending* to derogate him.

MEMO TO ME: Don't lose your temper, ever!

MEMO TO ME: Easy to say, hard to do.

June

8 Friday

Based on her last performance in my office, I was half expecting Michelle Sherborne to be dressed as a belly dancer with an emerald in her navel. However, I was disappointed. She was in a dark blue thing which covered her from her chin to well below her knees. And this time she didn't come round my desk and practically sit in my lap, either; she sat in a chair across the desk from me and stayed there.

What she has done in a fairly short time is creditable. She ran quickly through the gist of the talk she wanted to give, and showed me a set of overhead projector transparencies which fitted in with what she wanted to say and which were really professionally done. She said, 'What do you think, Tom? Will that go down all right?'

I said, 'Fine. It's exactly what's needed.' I meant it, too. 'I wish I could get my OHP transparencies as good as yours.'

She said, 'Oh, please let me do them for you, I'll be glad to.'

'Heavens, Michelle; I can't load you with a job like that.' But I wanted to, because I hate doing the damn things.

She said, 'But I like doing them, and it's my job anyway, since we don't have an advertising department.' So we arranged that when I had the information ready I would pass it to her for putting on to transparencies. She got up to go and stood for a moment smiling at me. She said softly, 'I came on to you too strongly last time, didn't I, Tom? Never mind; easy does it. I'm *so* looking forward to Ireland.'

Then she left, leaving me staring at the wall.

June

11 Monday

This morning Dorcas returned my greeting when I walked into her office and cocked her head at my door. 'Early visitor for you – very early. He was waiting outside when I arrived at 7.30 this morning.'

I said, 'Someone is keen this morning. Who?'

'Mr Milburn. I bring coffee?'

'No.' I saw no reason to give Ken refreshments, no matter why he had decided to honour me with a visit.

Ken had obviously prepared his speech and learnt it off by heart, which is usually a mistake because you invariably trip over yourself. The gist of his stammerings was that he and Joanne had talked it over at the weekend and they had decided that the present situation was fine and that they would like it to continue.

I said, just to drive it home: 'You want to keep your job here, then?'

'Oh, yes, Tom.'

'You don't want to resign?' All right, it was brutal, but I had been all the way there and back with this wimp.

'Oh, no, Tom.'

'Fine, Ken. Now all that nonsense is behind you, let's see a distinct improvement in performance and attitude.'

'Oh, yes, Tom.'

'Starting from today. You have an hour's drive before you reach your first customer. Move it.' He did the startled rabbit act again.

Dorcas appeared. 'This time Mr Milburn was leaving like Ayrton Senna. All repaired?'

'Fixed. Yes.'

'Thank you. Fixed. Now I make coffee.'

107

June

13 Wednesday

Extraordinary thing. Barry Leake walked in with an order from Pickering Plastics – it's the first time they have ever bought from us. Now, I knew that Barry had been after Pickerings for months, and I also know that Barry never gives up on a prospect; once he has his teeth in, he never lets go. This may sound like a good thing in a salesman and mostly it is, but there have been times when I have had to say to Barry, 'Listen, mate; you are never going to sell to that crowd. Now stop beating your head against the wall and spend your time more profitably with other prospects.'

Nevertheless, Barry is a good salesman and I wish I had more of his ilk. I congratulated him on the Pickering order and said I hoped it was the first of many. Barry said, 'Gerald Pickering himself told me that we could expect them to be regular customers from now on, but the crazy thing is *why*. I don't deserve the credit for this order, Tom. Let me tell you about it.'

As I said, Barry has been trying to get Pickerings for a long time without success. The trouble was mainly that Gerald Pickering, who is no fool, had tested our products against the opposition, and for his application there truly was no difference. It happens like that sometimes; we all like to think that we have the best product range and that everyone else has a lot of junk. The truth is that in these high-technology times there is often little or no difference between products in their performance on the job. The good salesman looks for the little difference and goes out and sells it, but sometimes it isn't easy to find. That isn't negative thinking, it's realistic.

So, Gerald Pickering saw no reason to change, or even to split his buying between the opposition and us. Now comes the interesting point. Pickering Plastics' factory is the pride and joy of Gerald

Pickering. The building isn't big, but the factory is always immaculate, and there are even flowers bordering the drive. On Monday Gerald Pickering phoned Barry to give him the order, the first ever, but he warned Barry not to get too excited because it was a one-off, never to be repeated. The opposition had run out of a certain type of co-polymer and Pickering was using us as an emergency supplier.

Well, it was better than nothing, and the order was delivered yesterday. This morning Gerald Pickering phoned to say that from now on we would be supplying fifty per cent of his film needs, and he told Barry why. (This is where the story gets hard to believe, but Barry swears that it's true.)

The driveway around the Pickering factory is a little narrow, and occasionally trucks delivering stuff to the rear put a wheel over the edge – right into the flowerbeds which are the apple of old man Pickering's eye. This gets his gastric juices working overtime, although it isn't really the fault of the driver.

So our driver delivered the product on Monday and, Murphy's Law, he put a wheel into the flowerbed. Gerald Pickering saw this through his office window and had to take antacid pills. On his way out our driver stopped the truck at the exit gate and went to the reception desk. He asked, 'Have you got a spade I can borrow?'

The receptionist had never had that sort of request before. She said, 'A spade? What on earth do you want a spade for?'

Our driver said, 'I went over the corner of the flowerbed. I want to fix up the damage.' After much searching around they found a trowel, since he obviously wasn't leaving until he got one, and the next thing that Gerald Pickering saw from his office window was the driver carefully digging away at the flattened earth and plants. Five minutes later he was on the phone to Barry. As Barry told it to me, he said, 'Nobody has ever bothered to fix the damage to the plants before, and if that is the sort of person who works for Hutton Horner, then they deserve a share of my business.'

I shook my head in wonder. I said, 'Well, you know where you are going right now, don't you?'

'Yes. I'm going down to Dispatch to ask old man Woolley which of his drivers it was. He is getting a bottle of Scotch paid for by me.'

I said, 'Put it on expenses. I'll okay it.'

Barry grinned. '*You'll* okay it, but will Mrs . . . will your secretary pass it?'

MEMO TO ME: Remember to get Barry to tell this story at the sales conference. Sometimes when products seem to be the same as the opposition's, it's the little things that make the difference. Quick exercise for the delegates – in ten minutes, put on paper ten things which make our products different. Have the delegates read them out, put them on the whiteboard, and let's see how many of the points relate to *service*.

June

14 Thursday

As I left home this morning Annabel said, 'Don't forget the PTA meeting tonight.' Damn it, I *had* forgotten. Annabel says it has been scientifically proved that one forgets the things one doesn't want to remember.

I hate PTA meetings. Balancing cups of milky tea and chocolate digestives in one hand and shaking hands with anonymous people with the other. Long discussions about whether to introduce mini-tennis and riding lessons.

I spent part of the day thinking of ways to duck out of it. I could phone and say that I couldn't get away; I often do get home later than the time of the meeting. I gave up the idea because (a) it would be a dirty thing to do and (b) Annabel would see through it in a flash.

We went and I survived. Oh, tell the truth, Liskeard; for once you actually enjoyed it. Firstly, there was a good sherry if you didn't want tea, and then Pete's form teacher is obviously very good at her job and a most interesting person to talk to. She said that Pete is a fascinating character with lots of imagination and with a creative bent. She said, 'He does tend occasionally to wander off into space, and I have to bring him back from a million miles away,' and laughed.

Annabel said, 'Yes, he's his daddy's boy, all right.'

MEMO TO ME: You are not in a nine-to-five job, and there are times when you can't get to PTA meetings and children's parties. But don't duck your responsibilities; you are not married to Hutton Horner, you are married to Annabel, who has just brought you an espresso which any Italian would kill for.

June

29 Friday

Out in the field all day with Wendy Carlton and, oh, boy, she is going to make it as a sales person. She hasn't been in her territory very long of course, and it was only the second time she had seen the people we called on. Still, she is making a good impression with her customers, and I can see why. She comes across as really wanting to help her people; she doesn't give the impression that she is only there to get an order and if one isn't forthcoming then 'the hell with you, Charlie'. She is a good listener, too, and she is quite disarming about the fact that she has a lot to learn and – and this is one that I have never heard a sales person use before – she makes it quite clear that since the customers know a lot more than she does, she expects to learn from them!

It shook me when I heard her say this to Stan Stanwick, one of our long-standing customers and something of a tough guy, but he looked at me and laughed. He said, 'Liskeard, you have a really keen one here. All right, young lady; don't ever try to fool me, give me good service, and I'll teach you about plastics!'

Come lunch-time and she was all for grabbing a sandwich and eating it on our way to the next customer. I said, 'Don't do it. There will be times when you are battling to get figures and every minute counts, or you are badly behind schedule and trying desperately to keep up. Then you may well miss lunch altogether and just keep going. But this isn't one of those times. We have put in a full morning's work and we need the break. Otherwise you can find yourself running out of steam by four o'clock this afternoon.'

So we sat in the park and ate tandoori take-aways. She said, 'Tom, you will tell me if you find me doing something wrong, won't you?'

I said, 'Certainly; that's why I'm out here with you.'

'But you won't take it easy on me because I'm a female? I would hate to think that you wanted to come down hard on me when I did something stupid, but you took it easy because I'm me and not Brian Hook, for instance.'

I was about to deny vigorously that I would do any such thing, but she was looking straight at me and something in her eye made me pause. I said, 'Wendy, I'll tell you. I have never had a woman on my sales team, and you could say that from that point of view I'm as new on the job as you are. All I can say is that I will honestly try to treat you in exactly the same way as the others. If you think that I'm failing in that, I want you to tell me. Okay?'

She said, 'Okay, Tom. Thank you.' I get the feeling that Wendy is a slightly humourless character, but that could simply be because she is trying to make a good impression. Out of harness she might be much more relaxed, and we'll see in Ireland if that is so. I like to watch my team at play as well as at work; I get a much better idea of the whole person that way.

We put our cartons in the rubbish-bin and walked back to the car. Wendy had something else to get off her chest. She said, hesitantly, 'Tom, I know that I didn't do as well as I might have on some of the calls this morning, but it's not so easy when – ' She stopped.

I helped her out. 'When I'm there?'

She said, 'Yes. Now, please don't take this wrongly – '

'Wendy, let me put you out of your misery. One of the first things a Sales Manager has to learn is that when he goes out with his people on calls, he is like an albatross around their necks. There is no way you are going to give of your best in front of a customer when you know that I am right behind you and listening to every word. Tomorrow you will be doing much better than today simply because I won't be there playing gooseberry. I know this, and I discount any nervousness or tension that I see in you or any of the boys.'

And of course as a result of that little chat she was much less nervous this afternoon, and did very well for a novice. She didn't crack any new accounts, which would have been expecting far too much, but she did show an old customer a product which he had never bought from us and got a small trial order for it. She was delighted. 'Wow! How about that, now! That was creative selling wasn't it? You talked about it when we went out the first time. Wasn't that creative selling?'

Her delight was infectious. 'You bet it was creative selling.' It was the last call of the day. 'Come on, I'll buy you a drink to celebrate your creative sale.' Over her gin and tonic she relived the calls we had made during the day, saying that she should have said this and done that, and that was good and the other was even better, and the next time she called on that customer she would show him the blister-packs – she was on a high, the adrenaline was still pumping, and listening to her took me back to my first days in the field as a cub salesman, and made me remember the exhilaration at the end of a really successful day.

That is what it is all about. Never mind all the tests by the recruitment agencies, the interviews, the application forms, all the nonsense questions about how old, male or female, what previous experience, where did you go to school and all the other bullshit surrounding the hiring of a sales person – forget all that. Give me someone who can get hyped up simply by doing the job well, who is actually *stimulated* by making calls and selling, and I don't care if he has two heads and walks on his knuckles. Give me a couple of dozen of those bodies and I will conquer the world in any field of selling you like to name.

All right, Liskeard; now get off your *own* high and go to bed.

July

3 Tuesday

I am not paying attention to my MEMOS TO ME. When I went out with Brian Hook the first time I was worried, and I wrote myself a memo telling me to watch him closely. I haven't been doing so.

I am sitting in my hotel room in Bodmin and staring at nothing instead of watching television or reading Jack Higgins, and it is Brian who is the cause of this. I went out with him today and my entry on May 9, when I wrote that I wondered if I had a problem with Brian, is now answered: I do have a problem. What is keeping me from *Cagney and Lacey* or Higgins's latest is that I don't know exactly what the problem is and it is making me go over my cigarette limit for the day.

What is wrong with Brian? Well, there is quite a lot which is *right* with him. He has exactly the right approach to customers; courteous, a little deferential, as befits a new salesman in an unfamiliar territory. He projects a good image of the sort of salesman we want in Hutton Horner. He doesn't waffle and he doesn't waste the time of the customer. He takes his leave gracefully.

That's what is right. What is wrong is that he doesn't really get inside the customer. He seems to have no conception of what a salesman's job consists of when he is face to face with a customer. I have just read over that and it isn't put very clearly but that is as near as I can get to it. Lack of a sense of direction in the presentation? A feeling that it doesn't matter all that much if he gets an order or not? I'm in the irritating position of a doctor who knows there is something wrong with the patient because the symptoms are there, but can't put his finger on the ailment. After all my time as a salesman in the field I should be able to diagnose the illness, but I can't.

Another thing. I told Wendy Carlton that all sales people are nervous when they give a presentation in the presence of their Sales

Manager; Brian shows no signs of nervousness whatever. Now, this is natural with one of my experienced men – Barry Leake, for instance, actually likes to have me with him on calls – but it is a little unusual for a brand-new boy.

Hell, that sounds as though I *want* them to be nervous when I go out with them, and that isn't so at all. I would like to feel that there is a little tension, though; the sort of thing a tennis player would feel when walking onto the court to play the singles finals. Barry doesn't have that. Can you be *too* relaxed in a sales presentation? Yes, I'm sure you can.

Well, I have another half-day with him before I have to leave for home. What can I say to him over breakfast that will put some fire into him?

Pete and Angie will be asleep by now; time to phone Annabel and say goodnight.

July

5 Thursday

Back in the office. People say, 'Hello. Did you have a good trip?' Not
that they care. It's just something that is said. I say, 'Fine, thanks.' It
wasn't a fine trip but you say 'fine', just as you say 'fine' when the
waitress asks you how the meal was. The fish had bones in it, the
salad was wilting, the coffee was muddy; you say, 'Fine!'

I have begun to realise just how far a manager sticks his neck out
when he hires someone, no matter what the job may be. Tell someone, 'All right, you are hired,' and you could be opening up a
Pandora's box of troubles. You haven't merely hired that person,
you have practically taken marriage vows with him. For better or
worse, you are stuck with him.

Getting rid of someone you hired because he isn't up to scratch is
not so easy. He is almost like a squatter in your house: only too easy
to acquire, a real headache to get rid of. Not that I am thinking of
getting shot of Brian Hook – at least not yet. It hasn't got to that stage
and perhaps it never will, but my visit to his territory has left me
feeling uneasy.

At breakfast on the day I had to leave I tried to put some mustard
into him. One of the things that worried me about Brian was that the
first thing a new salesman wants to know at the end of the day with
his manager is how his performance was. How did he do? Now
perhaps they don't always ask me right out, but they certainly want
to know my opinion of them. Brian didn't ask me and when I got
down this morning to giving him a brief evaluation of the previous
day he was polite, but he didn't really seem all that interested.

I said, 'Brian, you have a lot of things going for you,' and I
enumerated them. He nodded as he ploughed through his scrambled
eggs. 'But there are one or two other things. You are doing a good job
of showing your products, explaining them, even demonstrating

117

them – but you are not *selling* them, and that's why you are not producing any new business. The orders you are bringing are from customers who were established by your predecessor.'

He said, 'Oh, yes.'

'Now, that's fine, and nobody expects you to set the Thames on fire in your first few weeks, but you must keep your eyes open for new applications for old products and, when you see them, hit the customer with a strong sales presentation.'

He said, 'Oh, yes.'

'I know that down here in your territory you have to look after both Rigids and Flexibles and the range is wide, but yesterday at the Save 'n' Carry supermarket there was a chance of a sale for sink tidies staring right at you, and you didn't even mention it to the buyer. It could have been an easy sale. Now, Brian, let's really hit the ground running this morning. Find the need and go hard for the sale.'

He said, 'Oh, yes.'

I gave up. What can I do? Watch his figures, returned stock, slow payers, bad debts, paper work, expenses and all the things that go to make up a salesman who is in control of his territory. Schedule another trip down there not later than two months from now.

Damn it, Brian Hook; I am going to make a salesman out of you if it kills us both!

July

12 Thursday

I am dead-dog tired. I am bone weary. I am bushed. As I walked in this evening, Annabel went past me like an express train, gave me a micro-second kiss and said, 'Hard day, darling?' and kept going with her arms full of ironed washing.

The thing is, I *didn't* have a hard day. I am exhausted because today was one of those days when I didn't do a single damned thing.

Everyone in business knows that this is true. On the days when I am flat out, working at a hundred miles an hour, with callers, decisions, phone calls and letters coming at me right and left, I come home tired, certainly; but I am exhilarated, because, gee, I *did* things today!

Then there are days like today. I was there behind my desk as usual, and if you had looked into my office you would have seen me bent over papers; but nothing *happened*. When the curtain came down on the day and Dorcas took her leave, I couldn't point to a single thing and say, 'I accomplished that today.'

Those are the wearying days. This was one of them. Thank God there aren't too many of them. Phooey; let's have another drink. I deserve it – for doing nothing today.

July

16 Monday

Oh, poop. Appraisal time has come around. This is something that D-M instituted three years ago because he had attended a senior management conference where he was told that a working appraisal system was one of the most effective management tools any company could possibly have. Everybody goes through it from Directors to Ellen the tea-lady, and it is not the most popular thing that happens in Hutton Horner.

I see its obvious worth, but this is the first time I have had to do it myself. I have to put everyone in my team through it and the prospect frightens me a little. This is the formal appraisal, not the brief, one-page things I do when I go out with my sales people and evaluate their performance after one day in the field; that I don't mind doing at all. But this is a full four-page thing, with the person sitting opposite me, and we go through each item together. What if I do an appraisal on one of my people – especially one who is not only older than me but who has been in the company three times as long as I have – and he or she disagrees with my ratings and starts an argument? Are we going to end up in a knock-down, drag-out fight?

As a last resort, I read the instructions. Bert Corley left behind a book on management techniques. I look up 'Appraisal and Evaluation'. The magic words say: 'Do not enter into an argument with the appraisee on the subject of his gradings. By all means be prepared to justify your markings but do not defend them.'

The book gives an example: 'If, for instance, you rate an appraisee low on "Relationships with Fellow Employees" and he challenges you, you must be able to point to specific instances where friction and conflict have arisen which were undoubtedly initiated by the appraisee'.

Makes sense. If I tell Jock Nairn that his credit control is substandard – which it bloody well is – then I had better have chapter and verse to back it up. He already thinks that I'm a Sassenach upstart, and it could start an across-the-border feud that could last all my time with HH.

No doubt about it, the appraisal system is a good idea. Employees have a right to know what their manager thinks of them and they can't be expected to improve their weak points, or capitalise on their strong points, unless they know what they are. It's a fine thing, and the only thing wrong with it is that people tend to think of it in a negative way, as though they were back at school and have been told to report to the Head for a dusting down.

Well, it's up to me to show every one of my people that what we are going to be doing in the appraisal interview is intended to make them better at their jobs and, therefore, more valuable to the company *and* to themselves.

I'll be doing the Central team in a few days, and the outlying people later, as they assemble in London before flying over to Ireland. I've sent out duplicate appraisal forms to every sales person; they have to rate themselves before they sit down with me and go over the two forms – theirs and mine – together.

Oh, it is a very good idea; I just hope I'm up to doing it properly. I can see why so many managers dislike appraising and will do anything to get out of it.

Come on, chicken-lickin' Liskeard; what are you afraid of?

July

25 Wednesday

Had a brilliant idea about my motivation graph today. I see that it has been nearly two months since I put anything in the diary about it, but it has been wandering around in my mind ever since then; I don't have original thoughts like that so often that I can afford to let them go easily. Today at work I drew a line on a piece of paper, as I had done before, with plus 100 on top and minus 100 at the bottom. Then I put in four sample bars to illustrate the degree of positive or negative attitudes in people, like this:

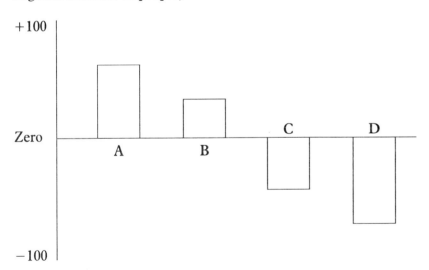

Now – and this was my brilliant idea – suppose you wanted to show whether they were getting better or worse? In the graph above, A is good, B is just over average, C is not so good and D is awful. But suppose you find that A, having been a fairly consistent worker, is now beginning to turn in a substandard performance and you track it

122

down to his attitude towards his job? Suppose that you find to your delight that the work you have put in with C has resulted in his performance improving significantly? Well, let's put arrows in the bars to show where they are *going* from where they are *now*:

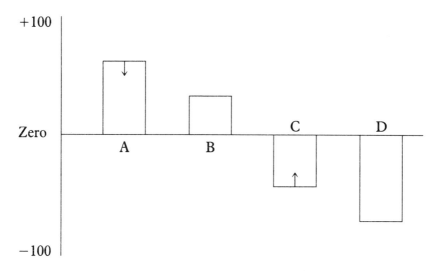

Something like this would help managers keep track of their people. They could move in the moment they saw something like the situation with A, for instance, find out what the problem was and stop it before it got out of control. As for C, here too something must be done quickly. C is showing improvement; so fine, let's recognise it, encourage C and jolly him along until before we know it he is above the ZERO line and is turning into an asset to the company.

All right, I know that this graph isn't perfect yet but the idea is sound. I'll keep kicking it around in my head. After all, I'm a Sales Manager; it isn't as though I have anything else to *do* all day, said he sarcastically.

July

27 Friday

I forgot to record that Annabel waved a card at me when I got home one day last week. 'Command performance. Invitation from the Dunsby-Martins to dinner next Friday. I haven't a thing to wear.'

I said, 'Oh, hell. From what I've heard about Elizabeth Dunsby-Martin it will be about as much fun as a documentary on Russian tractor manufacture.'

She said, 'Oh don't be such a wet blanket and anyway I've always wanted to see the inside of the Dunsby-Martins' house. Who else will be there, do you think?'

'I don't know. Maybe the whole management crew, maybe just us. This is something that D-M feels he has to do, just as we feel we have to accept. It will be a godawful evening.'

'That is a bad attitude, soldier. Get your mind straight. Now let's see, if I wear my blue dress I'll need some French-navy stockings . . .'

So this evening we duly presented ourselves at the Dunsby-Martins, together with, as it turned out, the Don Thorpes and the Mac McLeods. It was a much better evening that I expected, which so often happens when you are not looking forward to something. Elizabeth Dunsby-Martin greeted us by widening her mouth three millimetres, which I supposed she thought was a smile. D-M proved to be a very good host, as I would have expected. He managed, without seeming to try, to bring everyone into the conversation. Either he remembered that we had a boy and a girl, or he had peeked into my personal file before the party; anyway, he asked Annabel how they were and got on her right side immediately.

The life of the party was Ishbel McLeod. She was a large and very jolly Scots lassie who laughed at everything while Mac looked at her with adoration in his face. Amazing how different people are when you take them out of their working environment and put them in a social situation.

Some time in the evening Adele Thorpe grabbed my arm. She nearly knocked my eye out with an ice-blue creation with spangles and sequins or whatever – shiny little things all over the front of her dress. She had a complaint, and apparently it was all my fault. 'Mr Liskeard! What's all this nonsense about having this seminar of yours in Ireland of all places!'

She caught me on the wrong foot and for a moment I didn't know what she was getting at. My first reaction was to think, what the hell has it got to do with you, sourpuss? She went on, 'Don tells me that he will have to be away for five nights!'

The penny dropped; she didn't want her beloved to be away from her side for a single moment. I couldn't see why – if I were married to Don, I'd be happy to see him leave for six months on a trip to the Arctic Circle, but everyone to his or her taste. Then I did Don Thorpe a favour which he will never know about. It was on the tip of my tongue to say, 'It's not five nights, it's only four.' I stopped myself just in time. You owe me one, Thorpe. If there is something you wish to do on that extra night which you need to keep from your ever-loving, then it has nothing to do with me. *Buono appetito*.

Coming back in the car, Annabel was humming something catchy. 'What's that?' I asked.

'That is the *pas de quatre* from *Swan Lake*, you ignorant peasant. Wasn't it a nice evening? I enjoyed myself.'

I said, 'Well, you were the best-looking bird in the room, so naturally you enjoyed yourself. Yes, it was okay. What did you think of Medusa Dunsby-Martin?'

Annabel hit my arm. 'That's not a nice thing to say, Tom. Liz is a – '

'*Liz*? How did you get so chummy with her?'

'She asked me to call her Liz. She's a very shy person.'

'Shy? She's not shy, she's toffee-nosed.'

Annabel sighed. 'Tom, you are wrong. While we were powdering our noses, she said that she was so pleased to have met me and to find that I was so nice and friendly. She said she loves to have people come and call, but that it always terrifies her when she has to meet people for the first time. She's coming to tea next week; she wants to see the children. Poor woman, she can't have any of her own, and both she and Harold wanted them so much.'

My marriage will last for a thousand years because I shall never be able to take my wife for granted. She is so much better than me with people that she should go to work and do my job and I should stay at home and burn the food and break the dishes and scorch the ironing.

MEMO TO ME: Once and for all, Liskeard, will you stop making superficial, snap decisions about people. If you can be so wrong about D-M's wife, how can you be trusted to deal with twenty-three sales people? And, oh my gawd, appraisals coming up, too.

July

31 Tuesday

I have just come back from the first session of 'Finance for non-financial people'. All right, I agree that it is something I should do and I'm glad to be doing it at last, but it is not going to be a laugh-a-minute thing, as I can tell after only one session. The lecturer is hardly a typical accountant (if there is such a thing; I'm wary of type-casting people after my wife showed me up recently). He is an enormous bloke with big hairy arms – looks like an East German shot-putter. But when he started talking I would have known his profession if I had been next to him, blindfolded in a coalmine. They are all so bloody *precise*. Goes with the job, I suppose.

Oh well, one session down, seven to go, and then I shall be able to understand Don Thorpe. Is it worth it?

August

1 Wednesday

August already and the sales conference is just around the corner. As I have noticed before, when preparing for something like this, the big things give no trouble and the little things give nothing but trouble. We got a company to make everyone shirts with the HH logo and the slogan for the conference printed on the front ('GO FOR THE GOLD!'). Today they wrote and said that the shirts will be delivered ten days later than the promised date and they hoped that this will cause us no inconvenience. Hell, no! By then the conference will be over and everybody will be back at work, but who cares about that?

Now this is where Dorcas is worth her weight in rubies. She lifted the letter from my fingers and said, 'I see to it. The shirts will be there, I promise you. You are not to worry.' Later I walked through her office and heard her on the phone explaining to the Marketing Director of the shirt company why he was going to ensure personally that the garments in question would be delivered as promised. She sounded like Catherine the Great on one of her bad days, and the effect was enhanced by her losing her English for a moment here and there and putting in French, German and Hungarian – I suppose Hungarian – words in its place.

She said nothing to me and it was only this afternoon that I remembered the shirt problem and asked her if she had managed to sort it out. She said, '*Natürlich*. I explained the situation and the man was most co-operating.'

'Co-operative.'

'Thank you. Co-operative. I make coffee.'

I'm not surprised that the man was most co-operating. If I were that Marketing Director, after a talk with Dorcas I would be working one of the sewing machines myself to make sure the shirts arrived on time.

That sort of thing is why I prize Dorcas so much. Why should I

128

spend time chasing suppliers when I have someone who can do it better than me? And it isn't only the shirts; Dorcas has her desk covered with a hundred things to do with the conference. How she manages to keep her hand on everything I don't know, but she does. It was Dorcas who noticed that the sample for the name-tags was much too small. 'What is the use of names on people's chests if other people have to bend in half to see?'

The trick is to know exactly what you can leave to an assistant and what you have to do yourself. I happened to see a diagram of the main conference room on her desk. She had neatly drawn in the tables and was busy putting in the seating plan. I realised that I hadn't briefed her on this. I said, 'Hang on, Dorcas. That won't work. This is a classroom layout, with the tables in rows like the desks in a school.'

'So? Are they not learning like *l'école?*'

'Maybe, but they are not just sitting and listening, they are also supposed to talk and participate – and people talk when they can see each other. We need a U-formation, with the tables around the sides of the room.'

She saw the problem at once. 'Will need a bigger room for that.'

I said, 'Yes. The U or "horse-shoe" layout is wasteful of space, but we must have it.' I walked away and left her to it and she was on the line to the conference centre in Dublin before I was seated at my desk. Her head appeared in a minute. 'They have a bigger room for us. No puzzle.'

'Problem.'

'Thank you. Problem.'

'Thank *you*, Dorcas. You are a jewel.'

'The Cullinan diamond, surely. I make coffee.'

Anyway, things are slowly coming together. I had a mini-conference in the boardroom with all the people who would be speaking at the conference. I felt a little like a lieutenant ordering the staff officers about (since they were mostly older than me) but I bit the bullet and carried on. This is my conference, after all, and I am the one who is going to be judged on how it goes.

I stressed the necessity of keeping the time-table sacrosanct and recommended that all the speakers rehearse their speeches and time them to make sure they didn't run over. I warned them to expect questions from the floor. Don Thorpe said, 'Oh, there are never any questions.'

I said, 'I'm sure there will be this year.' I am too, for the simple reason that I am going to prime some of my sales people to ask questions. If necessary I shall even give them some questions to ask, although management won't know this.

I asked the speakers if they would be using any conference aids – slide projectors, overhead projectors, blackboards, white-boards, flip charts or felt boards. All of them except D-M said yes, they would be using the overhead projector. I said, 'Fine. Unless you are an expert in preparing transparencies, please let Michelle Sherborne have your material well in advance. She will produce really professional transparencies and take that job off your hands.'

Thorpe said, 'My secretary prepares mine.'

D-M said, 'Don, last year your figures were so small nobody could see them. Let Michelle do them.' Which made my day, no matter what else happened.

Then I gave them a short guide to using the overhead projector – never leave it on a second after you have used it to illustrate a point; you can't compete with the picture and people watch the screen and don't listen to you. Don't walk through the image; you look stupid with figures all over your face. Switch it off before you take one transparency off and put the next one on; it looks more professional that way. The group looked a little po-faced when I started telling them how to use something which they had all been using for years, but I sailed on. Damn few people use the overhead projector properly and it can make or break a talk.

I ended by saying that I didn't expect them, as speakers, to sit through all the sessions which they were not directly involved in, but if they wished to they were welcome – so long as they came in and left at the start and finish of each session, and not half-way through. Anyone in the room when a session started stayed there until it was over.

It went off all right, I thought. Anyway, D-M smiled and nodded when I thanked them for coming to the mini-conference and hoped that they would enjoy the conference itself.

Not long now, and I'm really looking forward to it. Partly (and I admit this only to the diary) because I can come out of this smelling like a rose. But only partly. If all goes well I really think that it will get the sales team on a high which will last most of the way through the year and if this happens it will definitely have an effect on sales.

Go for the gold!

August

6 Monday

Annabel has reminded me that Wednesday is Dorcas's birthday. I said, 'Now, did you really think that I'd forgotten?'

She said, 'Yes,' which happened to be the truth, but I have a lot on my mind at the moment. She said, 'What are you getting her?'

I said, 'Flowers.'

'What else?'

'What else? Just flowers, damn it!'

Annabel was not impressed. 'Not good enough. You can't just phone a florist and expect that to do.'

I said, 'All right, love. Will you please get something nice and tell me how much – '

'Not a chance. How would Seraphita feel if I bought her the present instead of you?'

'She won't know. Honestly, I'm so busy right now – '

'She will know. I'll tell her.' So today I took some time off and went shopping for a birthday present for my aristocratic dogsbody. I found a Victorian brooch with what the jeweller called garnets which looked exactly like Dorcas. He asked if I wanted it gift-wrapped and in an excess of zeal I said no thank you. I went and chose some pretty wrapping paper *and* some ribbon *and* a card. Liskeard does things in style.

Hope she likes it.

August

8 Wednesday

She liked it. She loved it. She grabbed my face in both hands and kissed me. She said, 'It is beautiful, Tom! And I know that you chose it yourself, yes?'

I said, 'Certainly! Do you think that I would let anyone else choose your present?'

The very idea.

August

14 Tuesday

Nearly blew it today.

Dorcas came in looking concerned. 'A Mr Tidmarsh of Clewer Construction.' She lowered her voice. 'He seems to be infuriating.'

'Infuriated.'

'Thank you. Infuriated. I bring him in?'

I thought quickly. As I remembered, Clewer was in Artie Watford's territory; what was Tidmarsh doing here, and infuriated? Whatever it was, keeping him waiting was probably making him even more so. 'Show him in,' I said.

He did look unhappy. I said, 'Good morning, Mr Tidmarsh, I'm Tom Liskeard,' but as I said it I recognised him; I had met him on a trip with Artie.

'Yes, sir. We have met.' He certainly was not happy.

'I remember. With Artie Watford. What can I do for you, Mr Tidmarsh?'

He said, not raising his voice but making it very definite, 'You can take back your rotten product and reimburse me for the time and trouble it will take me to make good the damage!'

I said, 'That sounds very serious, sir. Watford – '

'Watford is apparently miles away and I require this matter to be settled today.'

He was still standing. I said, 'please sit down, Mr Tidmarsh, and give me all the details.' The details were serious, all right. Clewer Construction had used our 'Unda-tile' plastic to seal the roofs of ten houses they were building near Colchester. Last night it had poured with rain and this morning the ten half-built houses had soaking wet roof trusses and ceiling boards, which meant that the offending plastic would have to be stripped off and the roof allowed to dry before, in Tidmarsh's words, 'some *good* under-tiling can be put on – not from Hutton Horner.'

133

I know a crisis when I see one. It wasn't only the cost of the plastic, it was all the work and time entailed, and if Clewer hit us with the costs of new ceiling boards and time off for allowing things to dry – holy cow. I said, 'Mr Tidmarsh, are you going back to Colchester now?'

'Yes, I am. I have to calculate the exact cost of the damage.' *That* didn't sound too good.

I said, 'I'll be following you in half an hour and I shall have one of my technical people with me. If you could tell me how to get to the construction site?'

Tidmarsh raised his eyebrows. 'Well, you certainly seem to be taking this seriously. Colchester is a long way from here, you know.'

'Mr Tidmarsh, Clewer is a valued customer of ours and we intend to keep it that way. I am dropping everything until this problem is settled to your satisfaction.' I hoped I sounded businesslike without being smarmy.

When Tidmarsh had left, I went to see Mac and told him all about it. Mac shook his head. 'It couldn't happen, laddie; not with Unda-tile. Not if it was properly installed. That product has a safety factor of about three hundred per cent.'

I said, 'I know, but the thing is that Clewer has been using it for ages, so they must know how to put it on. Mac, I'm leaving for Colchester right away and I want to take Ron Aston with me. May I have him? It will take all of the rest of the day, I'm afraid.'

Mac blew out his cheeks and looked thoughtful. 'If it has to be, then so be it.' Mac always looks at any situation from the point of view of the good of the company, never of his own convenience.

So Ron and I headed for Essex and possible deep trouble. Ron was also adamant that Unda-tile was a fantastic product which had never given trouble if the installation instructions were followed. 'Perhaps they had some new guys working on it?'

'Well, let's see when we get there.'

Tidmarsh was waiting for us. He introduced us to the site foreman and my heart sank when he said, 'This team has been working with your product for nearly a year, and this is the first time it has failed them. Come and see for yourself.'

We put on hard hats and climbed up ladders past soggy and sagging ceiling boards which looked like expensive trouble for Hutton Horner. The site foreman pointed up to the roof, and there it was, the HH logo plain to see on the plastic. I turned to Ron, ready to pull down the Hutton Horner flag and surrender unconditionally, but he had left my side and was clambering up the trusses like a monkey, making for the highest part of the roof. He reached up and ripped some of the plastic away, looked at it and jumped down to where we were. He said, 'This is not our product. Unda-tile will never do *this*,' and he tore the piece of plastic in two. On the larger piece was the crossed swords trademark of our opposition.

Tidmarsh went red. He turned to his site foreman whose chin had fallen on to his chest. After a lively bout of embarrassed cross-talk and some yelling at men standing around below, it appeared that unknown to the foreman, the tilers had used up an odd roll of opposition under-tiling. To make matters worse they had not confined it to one house but had interleaved it with our product on all the ten roofs.

Tidmarsh didn't know where to look. To give him his due he apologised most handsomely, invited Ron and me to lunch which we politely declined, offered to pay the cost of our trip which we wouldn't hear of – just part of our service, sir – and promised to write to our Managing Director, complimenting him on the calibre of his staff and their attitude towards their products and customers.

Ron says he doesn't drink Scotch so he gets a bottle of brandy, as well as my grateful thanks for pulling us out of what could have been a very deep hole. I'm ashamed of myself for not having more faith in my products and for being too ready to take the customer's word for it.

MEMO TO ME: The customer is *not* always right. It doesn't mean that he's a liar; he may truly believe something which isn't so. Moral? Check, check and check again.

MEMO TO ARTIE WATFORD: Clewer Construction will be in a very compliant mood towards considering more of our product range the next time you call.

Quite a day.

August

20 Monday

Did my first appraisal interviews today. I feel much better now that I have been blooded. In fact, what was I worrying about? What I was worried about, and I see it clearly now that I have been through it, was the possibility of *confrontation* of some sort. I foresaw a situation where the salesman would scream blue murder that his marks were too low, I would get angry and yell right back at him that he wasn't worth any more than that, and before I knew what was happening a fight would start.

It wasn't like that at all. Pat Swallow was the first one and I suppose I had him in first becuase I knew that he would be easy. It's always nice to be able to tell one of your men that he is doing well. Pat was a little nervous when he came in and this surprised me; I'd thought that it was me who ought to be nervous. I told him that the main reason for appraisals was not to bitch about the past so much as to set targets for the future; also, didn't he feel that he had a right to know what I thought of his performance?

Pat relaxed immediately. It was obvious that he had never thought of an appraisal interview in that way. After that we had no trouble, except that I found that on the form which he had filled in on himself, he had often rated himself lower than I had. I did six interviews today, and it was weird to see that four of the men had at least a few of their marks lower than mine.

I am sitting here staring at that last paragraph and wondering why that should be, and it has finally hit me that it could be one of two reasons – or both of them. Either the appraisee is deliberately marking himself low so that I won't think he has an inflated opinion of himself and slap him down or, and I have an unhappy feeling that this might be it, I am marking too high. Now, why would I do this? Let's remember that I am not Samuel Pepys and nobody will ever read this diary but me, so let's be honest here. If I have marked higher than I should, is it because I want to go easy on the man, or because I want to avoid a fight with him?

I hope it isn't the second alternative and, honestly, I don't think it is. I gave some very low marks in some cases; it was not all sweetness and light. I had some hard words to say where they were justified, too. Ken Milburn, for instance, may have settled his grotesque domestic problems, but his work has not shown the improvement it should have. It is marginally better but still below standard, and he went out of my office today with a set of targets which he will reach within three months or bye-bye, and he knows it.

I've done only six and it may be too soon to tell, but I am beginning to see just how valuable this appraisal business can be if it is done properly. Once the blokes see that no threat is intended, that it is a positive and not a negative thing, they open up and talk quite freely. Some of them do, that is. Ken Milburn sat through the whole thing as though he was in a cell on Death Row. Artie Watford produced nothing but monosyllables – Lord knows why, since his ratings were mainly pretty good. Apart from those two, I really feel good about the interviews and I suppose the reason that I am sitting here writing more than I usually do is that I am filled with a mixture of satisfaction and relief. I found out things about people that I had never realised and that I would never have known without the appraisals.

For instance, Ben Frome likes prospecting for new business. He said that the best part about selling as far as he was concerned is tracking down new accounts. Now, that is fine and it is a very valuable characteristic in a salesman, but the problem is that Ben is on the Retail side, and Retail staff don't do much prospecting. It may be a thought to shift Ben to Industrial, where he can prospect to his heart's content.

Another interesting example: I congratulated Sidney Cornwell on his organisation – he was the only one I could give ten out of ten to for that category. He laughed and said, 'My wife Helen said that if you didn't give me full marks for that she would come in and beat you over the head!' It appears that every evening he and his wife sit down and she helps him to organise his paper work, plan his calls for the next day and work on his sales graphs.

I said, 'Give her my regards and say that I'm very impressed.'

He said, 'Oh, she likes to help. We are both ambitious for me to do well, and we reckon it's worth the little extra work.' Interesting!

Of course, soon now D-M will call me in and go over my own appraisal form with me. Worried? Why should I be worried? The appraisal interview is a *positive* thing, as I always tell my sales people.

August

22 Wednesday

Well, I have completed the appraisal interviews for the Central, Eastern and Southern districts and I am completely exhausted. They went well, just one or two that I thought I could have handled better. Anyway, I have learnt one thing which is that next year I am going to space them out over several weeks instead of trying to do them all in a few days. What happens, I found, when you do six or seven in one day, is that you actually mix up the people in your head, and you can't properly distinguish the strengths and weaknesses of the different men. And this with people that I know well! Several times I had to sit back and think: wait a minute, it's Victor I'm thinking of, not Mike.

I'll know better next time. Only the Northern and Midlands districts left, and I'll do them next week, before we all take off for the Emerald Isle. Except Eddie Blawith, of course, who will 'steam off' as Dorcas says. Since this is a conference in Ireland, wouldn't it be something if we all land safely, as we certainly will, and Eddie's ship sinks with all hands? Just kidding.

August

23 Thursday

I have been appraised, and I still have my job. Instead of calling me up to his office, D-M took the unusual step of coming down to mine. Courteous as ever, he asked Dorcas if it would be possible for her to hold Mr Liskeard's calls for half-an-hour, and could he, did she think, have some of her excellent coffee?

Looking back on the interview I see just how well D-M handled it. He managed to make it a conversation rather than an interview – interview as in 'interrogation' or even 'inquisition'. He went through the form almost, it seemed, talking to himself '"Attitude to company" – high ranking there, of course; you do like us. "Ability to work with company staff" – very high, Tom. It's one of your talents, that you get on with people.' He eyed me. 'You even manage to disguise your dislike of Don, in the larger interests of the company.' He made a note on the form. 'He's not a bad chap, you know.'

I felt myself going red. 'No, of course not.'

'Has an unfortunate manner at times. Incidentally, how's the financial course going?'

I said, 'Fine, D-M. I'm getting to grips with it now. I see how important it is to have that sort of knowledge. I know I have to be able to speak the language of accountants.'

'Weird fellows, are they not? Breed of their own. Have to have them, of course. Self-organisation – only fair on that one, I think, don't you?'

I said, 'Oh. You feel I'm lacking in organisation?'

'Lacking? No. I feel that you have to force yourself to get organised, that you don't have an instinct for it. However, it is not so serious a failing in you as all that. It doesn't seem to hamper your performance in any way. In any event, you have a marvellous built-in organiser in Mrs . . . your secretary.'

140

I wasn't sure that I was happy about being told that I was a scatterbrained twit but, thank God, my secretary would always put me right.

D-M went through a few more points, mainly complimentary, and said, 'That's that. Well done, Tom.' Then he asked an interesting question, and I am going to pinch it for use in future appraisals. He said, 'Tell me; is there anything in the company's policies or procedures, or anything in your day-to-day working situation, which could be modified or discarded in order for you to do your job more effectively?'

I think I have it down word for word, just as he said it. I don't know as many words as he does and I don't talk in the same way, so when I use it I'll probably say something like, 'Is there anything that I or the company can do to help you do your job better?' Different words but the idea is the same, and what a good question it is! Even if my sales people come back at me with something we can't do anything about, at least what is bugging them will be out in the open, and we can talk about it.

I looked at my boss and said, 'Well, D-M, you have just this moment thrown it at me. I can't think of anything right now. Certainly, nothing jumps out at me.'

He got up and smiled. 'Well, the question stands. As you know, I'm at your service should you think of something.' He nodded and left, and I heard him thank Dorcas for the coffee. The perfect gentleman, and I know it isn't put on like one of his club ties. With D-M it's instinctive.

Unlike my capacity for self-organisation. I realised that I had come out of the interview well, but that one remark of D-M's still rankled. I told Annabel about it and she laughed. 'He wants to come here and look into the garage. He'll learn something about your skill in organising things.' She went through to the kitchen.

Garage? What *about* the garage? I went outside and opened the garage door. Bag of fertiliser knocked over and spilling onto the floor . . . Rust on a saw-blade . . . Carpet tacks in a bottle marked 'Tap washers' . . . Lawn-mower bin half-full of grass cuttings . . .

I went back inside where Annabel was mixing Martinis. I said, 'I really am pretty awful at organising, aren't I?'

She gave me the stemmed glass and twisted lemon rind over it. 'Darling, you are the best and only husband I shall ever have, but you do rather slap at the mosquitos instead of draining the swamp.'

'Where on earth did you get that jargon? You hate that sort of talk.'

'From a novel I'm reading. Isn't it neat? And don't sulk, darling. Apart from that, how did the – what do you call it – the appraisal go?'

I sulked a bit more. I muttered, 'Excellent. D-M thinks I'm a terrific manager.'

'Except for organisation.'

'So who's perfect?'

'You are, darling.' She kissed my ear. 'Move over and I'll show you how perfect you are.'

Goody!

August

24 Friday

Last working day before we all leave for the conference, and the office should have been a madhouse. Why wasn't it? I sat at my desk, got up and walked around it and sat down again. I waited for the telephone to ring, people to come to see me, Dorcas to take dictation and some crisis or other to raise its ugly head, but nothing.

I got so lonely with nobody but Garfield to talk to that I went out and had coffee with Dorcas in her office. She sat back at ease with her feet in her bottom drawer, sipping coffee and clearly without a care in the world. I said, 'Dorcas, what's wrong? Why are we not rushing around frantically doing last-minute things?'

'Because there are no last-minute things to do.'

'Why not?'

'Because I am such a wonderful organiser.'

I groaned. I should never have told her about D-M's comment on her organising ability. I said, 'Damn it, there must be something I can do. I'm getting jail-fever in these four walls.'

'Getting your hair cut is what you can be doing; it is much too long. Much shorter, or else you should buy a guitar and join a roll group.'

'Rock group.'

'Thank you. Rock group.' The telephone rang. Dorcas answered it and said, 'Mr Hornsey. For you.'

I took it. 'Yes, Paul?'

Our Credit Manager said, 'Tom, I'm sorry to bother you when you are probably rushed off your feet with last-minute things, but I just wanted to confirm the dress in the conference room. Your memo says "casual". Do you really mean that? In the past we have always worn jackets and ties. What does "casual" mean – open-necked shirts?'

'Right, Paul. For the first day you wear the HH shirt which we sent you and no tie. The only time we go formal is the banquet on Wednesday evening.'

'And that's black tie?'

'No.' Why don't people read memos? 'Some of the delegates probably don't have dinner jackets and we didn't want them to go to the expense of buying one, so it's dark suits for the banquet.' Just as it says in the memo which you probably have lying on your desk in front of you, birdbrain.

'And it's everyone outside here at the main gate at 2.30?'

'Right; to be bussed to Heathrow.'

'For the 4.15 flight.'

'That's it. See you there, Paul.' I gave the phone back to Dorcas and made a face.

She said, 'Mr Hornsey likes to have everything exactly so.'

'Pernickety idiot.'

She said thoughtfully, 'Is going with the territory, I think. He has a pernickety job.'

'So he has. I forgive him.'

'Haircut.'

'I'm going, I'm going.' I had a thought. 'Annabel phoned and asked you to tell me to get a haircut, didn't she?'

Dorcas merely looked inscrutable. 'Shorter above the ears and also around your backside.'

I opened my mouth and then closed it again: backside would do.

August

25 Saturday

I don't believe it. Angie woke this morning with a runny nose and a temperature, which means that Pete will probably catch it from her and that means that Annabel will probably also get it, and the day after tomorrow I leave for Ireland – and this is one trip I simply cannot postpone.

Both children were miserable because I had promised them a proper restaurant lunch since I was deserting them for four days. I did the best I could; I went and got take-aways with ice cream and all the trimmings and we had a picnic around Angie's bed.

What bad luck. It's at times like these that I think of a job in a building society, where you get home at the same time every night and always sleep in your own bed.

August

27 Bank Holiday Monday

10.30 am

A quick note before I slip the diary into my briefcase as I pack for the trip. Angie has woken up this morning fit and healthy and full of bounce. Thank you, patron saint of Sales Managers, whoever you may be.

10.30 pm

And here we are in dear ould Oireland, begorrah, and so far, touch a leprechaun, everything has gone as smooth as silk. Everyone in time for the bus, no panic of any sort at Heathrow, another bus-ride out to the conference centre with the driver in a very good mood and telling Irish jokes over his PA. Then the centre itself, and it has turned out much better than I expected. D-M is smiling from ear to ear because he chose the place on the basis of a brochure and a couple of photographs, and you can go woefully wrong by taking that sort of chance. As it turns out the place is a beautiful mansion set in lovely grounds with a fabulous view. The bedrooms are large and bright, the conference room is a real surprise – very modern, with built-in projectors, whiteboards that slide away when not in use, back-projection screens – any trainer would kill for a conference room like this.

This evening we had an informal get-to-know-you drinks party where everyone had thirty seconds to introduce themselves. Some of the salesmen almost never get to head office and they didn't know everyone, especially the newer members of the team. Interesting to see how differently people do this. D-M started the ball rolling – as if anybody there didn't know who he was – by saying, 'Good evening. My name is Harold Dunsby-Martin, and I am the most important person in this room . . .', he paused for his punch-line,

146

'. . . because I'm signing the cheque for all this!' Which got his laugh and showed the delegates that they didn't have to be serious in the introductions. We wanted people to sing out their names, jobs (and territory if they were sales people) and length of service in HH. Some played it absolutely straight: 'I'm Reggie Plumstead, Central District Industrials, been with the company four years.' Some stuttered and blushed. Some, the extroverts, were noisy: 'I'm Neville Runford, been here two years, and I'm the best salesman in the Midlands District!' Practically a mini-appraisal of each one's personality.

After a light supper the old buddies got together in groups, playing snooker or table-tennis or simply sitting around renewing friendships. This is a valuable spin-off of these conferences, no question about it. I was idly watching a very inexpert darts match when I heard my name called. A group of the more experienced Retail boys were sitting over a table full of Guinness bottles, deep in argument. I was called in to give my opinion of tumble-pack displays as against gondola-ends, and I was soon as deeply involved as I would have been out in the field calling on customers. I wished that D-M would come into the room and see that sooner or later when you put good sales people together with their mates, they stop telling lies about their fishing exploits and start talking business. What the company was getting around that table was a lot of voluntary (and unconscious) overtime.

After I had had three pints of Guinness practically poured down my throat, I said, 'That's it for me, fellows. I don't have your tough constitutions.' I slipped away without making a big thing about saying good night to everybody.

I think that this is an important part of the manager–salesman relationship, especially on a residential conference like this one. On the one hand you simply have to muck in with everyone; it would be a disaster if I spent my after-hours time drinking gin fizzes with Mac or Don or Paul, for instance. On the other, there is a fine line between having a few companionable snorts with them and then pulling out, and staying drink-for-drink with them and ending up singing 'The Wild Colonial Boy' till all hours of the night.

What a lot of managers don't realise is that the team likes to have them around as part of the happy circle *for a certain time*. After that it is up to the manager to leave the staff to their own devices.

Which is why I am sitting propped up in my feather-bed, writing in my diary and trying to think of any little thing which still needs to be done before kick-off time tomorrow.

Oh, for chrissakes, Liskeard! If there was anything, then Dorcas would have it well under control. She is certainly sleeping peacefully next door, so why don't you pack it in and get some shut-eye.

Whatever else tomorrow may be, it shouldn't be dull.

August

28 Tuesday

Well the first day went quite well, I think, in spite of a slightly shaky start because we were three men short in the conference room at 8.30 when D-M was due to give the opening speech. D-M was ready to walk up to the lectern and there were those three empty seats. Dorcas disappeared and in two minutes the three men came in and sat down. I don't know where Dorcas found them or what she said to them, but they came in fast and looked properly chastened. Turned out they had decided to take a walk after breakfast, if you don't mind. Is it necessary to put '8.30 SHARP' on the programme? Anyway, it was a lesson to everyone there and I think we'll be starting on time from now on.

D-M's speech was quite different from last year's. Could my little chat to him of several months ago have had an effect? For whatever reason, it was very positive and encouraging. He made it his business to pick out a few names in the team who had done especially well and he had some nice things to say about me – 'who, in less than a year has shown a real talent for working closely with all of you. In fact, I can never find him when I need him – he is always out in the field with you people.' Without going overboard and embarrassing Wendy Carlton, he welcomed her appointment as a step in the right direction and said with a smile that her presence would raise the tone of the conference. The applause when he sat down was much louder and more prolonged than the usual light patter, and I breathed a sigh of relief that he had got the whole thing off to a good start.

Then came Don Thorpe's turn. I admit that Don doesn't have a very exciting subject to talk about; who can get worked up about fixed costs and variable costs and cash flow and idle stock and inventory control? Even so, Don's way of giving a talk would discourage a group of sailors at a strip-tease show. One thing which was a

149

big improvement on last year was his visual aids. The transparencies which Michelle had done for him made even his boring sets of figures worth looking at. I was holding a watch on Don and, to give him credit, he finished bang on time. I had deputed members of the sales staff to act as chairman for the conference, four for each day, each one handling one of the quarters: start to coffee, coffee to lunch, lunch to tea, and tea to close. I don't know where I got this idea from, but it worked out very well. Last year Bert Corley chaired the whole conference from start to finish and this meant that the group's Sales Manager was always up there on the platform in front of them. I didn't like this idea and I thought, no, it's the sales team's conference so let them chair it. Pat Swallow took the first session and he did well; I think he rather liked lording it over the Managing Director and the Financial Director.

Pat thanked Don for his talk and threw the meeting open to the floor. I had primed a couple of the blokes to ask questions, and Don, who had sat down with the air of one who has finished a good job, had to stand up again and be put over some high hurdles about the delay in getting expenses cheques out to the field and the practice of not sending receipts to customers who had specifically asked for them.

Interesting thing; after this question-and-answer session, there was a definite change in the attitude of the delegates. I could actually *feel* an increase in interest and attention, and that is really remarkable when you realise that it was a talk on accountancy which the group had been listening to. I am certain that the change was because people suddenly realised that on this conference they were going to be *heard*. They were not going to have to sit and take it, they were going to be able to dish it out, as well. No question about it, the atmosphere in the room was different.

It was after morning coffee-break that we really broke away from the conventional sales conference. We started with Barry Leake talking for fifteen minutes on the subject of service. When I had first told Barry that he would be addressing the entire conference and, not only that, he would be sandwiched in between talks by senior management, he went into shock. I sat down with him and we blocked out an outline of his talk. I reminded him of the incident of the truck over the flowerbed at Pickering Plastics, and his eyes opened wide when he realised that it was a classic case where service brought us business in a situation where product features by themselves could not.

Barry was a little nervous at first but he soon got into the swing of it. The flowerbed incident got a laugh, which I hadn't expected, but I could see from the nodding that the point had come across. Barry got an enthusiastic hand from his colleagues, and his grin showed that he had enjoyed his moment in the limelight.

What was really good was that several questions came from the floor after Barry's talk. I hadn't thought that there would be questions after the salesmen's talks, but it did show that there was a real interest in the subject. Barry answered one or two and then said, 'Hang on; I can't answer that one. Tom, this is your baby.' I took the floor very briefly, and answered the question; it was about what a salesman should and should not do in a customer's factory. I made the answer short, because I was much more interested in getting the group to talk rather than have them listen to me; they would get plenty of me in the three days.

The group took the ball back and threw it around until I began to worry about timing, and I caught the eye of David Lundy, who was chairing that part of the conference. I tapped my watch and David wound up the session very neatly, I thought, then introduced the next speaker.

I realised, sitting there, that there was a lot more to running a successful conference than I had thought, and I began to see that the job of people like Tweedledum and Tweedledee was not as simple as it looked from the outside. It's no great problem if you run a lecture-type meeting because there the poor audience has to sit and take it – or fall asleep – while the speaker reads from his notes. But if you have a format where you not only allow questions but actually encourage them, then immediately there is the problem of timing. What do you do if the group grabs hold of a subject which is of real interest and value to them? Do you chop them off in mid-stride and go on to a subject which is of less interest, in order to keep to the timetable? Or do you allow them to carry on and wreck the timing of the whole day? Don't ask me; I'm not an expert on conference management, I'm just a salesman. Something to ask the Proselling twins if I ever talk to them again.

I had put Paul Hornsey on the agenda for the first morning. I hadn't wanted to, since Accountancy and then Credit in the same session is like eating a boiled pudding with no filling, just the dough all the way through, but I really had no choice because Paul wasn't staying for the whole conference, but was going back home this afternoon. *Somebody* has to mind the shop.

Oddly enough, Paul's talk wasn't all that bad. Again, like Don's, it isn't easy to get on a high about credit control, but Paul kept it light, he didn't whine about incomplete credit reports, and he ended his talk by saying, 'Remember, fellows, that I hate turning away customers just as much as you do. Don't forget, the sales you make pay my salary as well as yours. So give me every bit of credit information you possibly can, and between us we will give every bit of credit that we possibly can.' Nice ending, and when David Lundy in thanking Paul said, 'I think every one of us can give an example of where the Credit department has bent over backwards to help us in the field,' Paul got a second round of applause. We had evidence that red blood does, contrary to rumour, actually flow in a Credit Manager's veins, because he blushed with pleasure.

I read somewhere that the toughest time in a conference of any sort is the hour before lunch, because the delegates have had a long morning and their blood sugar is low, and the hour after lunch, when people tend to be sleepy after the midday meal. This did happen. Not so badly that the conference fell to pieces, but the pace definitely slowed down between noon and the lunch break, and then from two to three. After that they all seemed to get a second wind. I may change the agenda slightly for tomorrow, to give them a high-participation session around lunch-time; keep them awake by making them talk.

Through my window I can hear the murmur of talking and the occasional burst of laughter, but it is nearly eleven o'clock and the boys should all be in bed by midnight. One of the many things I discussed with D-M before the conference was the policy on drinks. We agreed first of all that there would be a strict rule – no alcohol at lunch. In fact as far as the delegates were concerned, the bar was to be considered closed until six in the evening. That was no problem; the point at issue was, who pays? There are three ways to do this: one, any drinks are paid for by the delegates themselves, no bar cards to be signed. Two, same as number one but each delegate is given an allowance for drinks, say, £30 for the period of the conference, and he can do what he likes with it. He drinks Scotch and blows it all, or Coca-Cola and puts most of it in his pocket. Three, the company picks up the bill for all drinks.

At one of the pre-conference meetings I pushed hard for number three. I said, 'It will show the men that we believe that they will honour the trust that we have in them and that they won't overdo the drinks angle.'

Don Thorpe of course was against it in principle – if he has any principles. D-M thought about it and gave me the nod. He said, 'Let's try it this year. They will know that if they overdo it, then it will be the last time. Also, they surely know that they are being evaluated on the basis of their behaviour at the conference.'

Don Thorpe agreed reluctantly. He said, 'It might be wise to include in each person's conference package a note saying that everyone should recognise that a good deal of trust is being placed in them with this arrangement.'

I said, 'Is that necessary? If we trust them do we have to spell it out?'

But here D-M was on Don's side. 'Just a precautionary measure,' he said. 'You will know how to word it tactfully, Tom.'

So that is what has happened, and it seems that so far it is working.

I think that management often doesn't realise that a sales conference should, as well as getting all the information across to the sales people, also be a way of saying to everybody, 'We are going to be working hard during the day, but we stop at 4.30, and we expect you to enjoy yourselves, unwind, and have a good time with your colleagues and friends.'

The first thing I noticed when I joined Hutton Horner was that there was a sort of family spirit about the place. Generally, and allowing for the odd spat, people worked well together. In spite of the occasional difference of opinion, when there was a crisis, people closed ranks and battled it out as a family. I have always thought that this is very important, and a conference such as this can renew and nurture that spirit.

On that rather pompous note, Liskeard, you can put out the light and dream of Annabel, who assured you on the phone earlier that all the family are well, everything is fine, Pete confidently expects you to bring back a four-leaf clover, and that she loves you.

August

29 Wednesday

I am as furious as I can ever remember being. Just before 8.30 this morning there was one seat vacant, Jack Oxhill's. I asked if anyone knew where he was and there were a few grins and mutters. I asked 'Who is doubling up with Jack?' and Arnold Temple raised his hand. I went over to where he was sitting and he said in a low voice, 'Better carry on without him, Tom. He took on a few too many last night and he's still asleep.'

It was starting time and there wasn't a thing I could do. I couldn't very well ask Dorcas to go and pull him out of bed. To D-M's raised eyebrow I said, 'It seems he's not feeling so good. I'll check at coffee-time.'

I checked at coffee-time and then *I* wasn't feeling so good. Jack was still in bed, snoring his head off. A smell in the bathroom indicated that at some stage he had thrown up, but not very accurately. I went downstairs and tracked down the barman who said that the poor gentleman had taken a drink and had been ill on the steps outside the bar – could not hold his liquor at all, at all.

When I asked some of Jack's colleagues they were reluctant to put him deeper in the shit than he already was, but he had apparently resisted all attempts to get him to go to bed. There were broken glasses and a shattered lampshade to testify to his unwillingness to call it a day.

I told D-M at lunch break, and if I had had any idea of glossing over some of the ugly details, his immediate anger put that out of my mind. He asked, 'Is he awake now?'

I said, 'Yes, apparently he is getting washed and dressed. He'll be down for lunch, although whether he will feel like eating any-thing – '

D-M interrupted me. 'I want him out of here this instant.'

154

I was bewildered. 'Out of here?'

'He must not appear at lunch. I do not wish to see him appear at the conference.' D-M's face was like stone. 'Get him on the first aircraft back home.' He meant every word of it and I decided to do exactly as he said in an effort to save some of my own hide. I had the feeling, and sitting here writing this I still have it, that I am not going to get out of this with a whole skin. I was the one who said, 'Trust my salesmen. Pay for their drinks. They won't go overboard; they are responsible adults.'

I left Jack's flight arrangements to Dorcas and went up to his room. He had just had a shower and was using an electric razor. He grinned shamefacedly at me in the mirror. 'Sorry about this morning, Tom. Had a couple too many last night. Never mind, I promise I'll be a very good boy for the rest of the conference.'

I said, 'For you, there is no rest of the conference. You are booked on the afternoon flight back to London. Mr Dunsby-Martin's personal instructions.'

As the meaning behind my words hit him, Jack's face lost all its colour. He collapsed on to the loo seat and put his face in his hands. 'Oh, bugger it.' He looked up at me. 'I'm finished, aren't I?'

Standing there looking at him I realised just how angry I was. I said, 'The way I feel at the moment you are. I shall have to see what the MD says, but I'm not sure I want you in my team any more.'

He said, 'Just for getting a bit pissed? You'd lose a good man for that?'

I wanted to tell him that it wasn't just a question of a few drinks too many, it was letting the side down, and of course making me look like an idiot in the eyes of senior management. I wanted to say all that but I found that my hands had somehow become fists, and I knew that if I stayed in that room for ten seconds longer, I would hit him. I turned and left.

At two o'clock the delegates were settling down in their places and there were one or two comments about Jack's non-appearance, when something happened which shook everybody up. Evelyn Street, D-M's secretary, walked into the room, picked up Jack's place-card from the table in front of his seat and walked out with it. There was a dead silence. Evelyn wouldn't have done that off her own bat, of course; she had taken her instructions from her boss. Her action explained very clearly exactly what had happened and no further discussion was necessary.

Before dinner this evening I was sitting here in my room working on the sessions for tomorrow, when there was a tap at the door and

D-M walked in. He said, 'Spare me a moment, Tom?' Of course, I said, 'Certainly.'

He picked up my phone, asked for room service and ordered two gin and tonics. He chatted about the conference until the drinks came and when we had each taken our first sip he said, 'I came along to apologise, Tom.'

'*Apologise*, D-M?'

'Yes. That business with Oxhill today. I was . . . I lost control for a moment and usurped your authority. I had no right to take a decision about one of your men out of your hands in that way. I hope that you'll forgive me.' For the first time since I had known him, he was not completely composed.

I said, 'D-M, that's very generous of you, but I've been thinking about it and I realise that you did the right thing. I don't believe that you usurped my authority, as you put it; I think that you relieved me of a responsibility that I wasn't ready for. As you said yesterday, I've had this job for less than a year, and what happened with Oxhill was something I've never had to deal with before.'

D-M said, 'Have you thought how you might have dealt with it, had I not taken the reins from you?'

'I'm not sure. I might have torn a strip off him and waited until we got back home to make a decision as to whether to keep him or fire him.'

D-M said, 'Yes, that would have been a very natural reaction. However, it would have meant his attending the conference this afternoon. Had he walked into the room at two o'clock, what would the attitude of the other delegates have been, do you think?'

'Well, they would have pulled his leg, of course.'

'What would Oxhill have done?'

'Oh.' I thought for a second. 'He would have grinned and made a few funny remarks.' A light dawned. 'To some of the delegates he would have been a sort of a hero – a hard-drinking, macho type who doesn't have to turn up at the conference.' I shook my head. 'It would have been an impossible situation.'

'Unthinkable. Your authority would have been diminished. As it is now, he's gone, and soon forgotten in the hurly-burly of the conference. We have amputated the gangrenous member and the body is safe.' D-M likes the occasional colourful metaphor.

I said, 'So – is he dismissed?'

D-M inclined his head at me. 'Your decision, Tom. What do you think?'

I said, 'This morning I was so furious that I could have killed him with my bare hands. Now – I don't know. He was irresponsible and stupid rather than malicious. Perhaps being sent home in disgrace is enough punishment.'

D-M nodded approval. 'Good point. However, I think you will find that he will immediately start looking for employment elsewhere. Unless he is extremely dense, he must know that he has blotted his copybook with Hutton Horner. Watch now for his apparent compliance with all instructions and complete adherence to protocol. At the same time, notice that his sales figures will drop. He won't be working for you, he will be using the company's time and petrol to go job hunting.' D-M rose and said briskly, 'Well, Tom, that's over and done with. Thank you for this talk. Good-night. Sleep well.'

Just possibly, one day I shall have the same wisdom, foresight, judgement and sense. It comes with experience, I suppose.

One day older, five years smarter – I hope.

August

30 Thursday

Third and last day, and the conference is over. We have just had the farewell banquet, I am lying on my bed writing this, and if my hand isn't very steady then blame it on some glasses of white wine, some of red, and two cognacs. Let's see if I can get my thoughts in order; 8.30 this morning seems a long time ago.

First session was Mac McLeod's and he surprised everybody by calling his talk 'A day in the life of a Production Engineer'. He told us about the problems and the satisfactions of a typical day and, by golly, it was well done. Amusing, too – he had the whole room laughing at some of the things that happen in a factory. What most of the boys didn't realise was that he was getting a few commercials into the talk, like 'don't make unrealistic promises to customers about delivery dates', 'do make absolutely certain of specifications,' 'get the customer's signature on the colour sample itself, so that he doesn't come back at us screaming that the green is too dark' – that sort of thing. No doubt about it, his talk set the tone for the day. I have realised how important it is to *start* each day well. A dull session in the beginning and the whole gang is set to fall asleep the rest of the day; a good first speaker and we hit the ground running.

Next we had four of the sales team giving their fifteen-minute talks on various subjects – prospecting, opening new accounts, getting credit information without antagonising the customer, and the use of sales aids. They were less nervous than I thought they would be, probably because they saw that the audience was sympathetic and the tone was relaxed. I was pleased to see how much work they had put into their talks. I had the new boy, Brian Hook, acting as chairman for the talks and he was excellent. He jollied them along when they dried up, kept them to their allotted times, and handled the open sessions – questions from the floor – like an expert. Maybe

I have been wrong about him? He showed maturity and a very good attitude.

Talking about new people, I took a chance and gave Wendy Carlton one of the sessions. Her subject was, 'Is selling easier if you are a woman?' She came across quite well and the boys gave her a big hand at the end. I thought it was a good way for them to get to know her and it seemed to work well.

And on the subject of females, another good talk came from Michelle Sherborne. She had on a yellow tennis shirt, which was perhaps a little too casual for the conference, but when she started talking it was obvious that as far as her job was concerned she was a real professional. She got the whole room interested in PR, and the number of questions afterwards threatened to screw up the timetable completely.

After her talk it was lunch-time, and I sought her out to thank her for the talk and congratulate her on the way she had put it across. She said, 'Oh, I'm good, Tom. You don't know how good I can be.' Her hand was holding my arm.

I said, 'Yes, well, I just wanted to thank you.'

She moved closer, until my arm was touching the shirt and what was under it. 'You can thank me properly this evening.'

'Uh – yes.' There didn't seem to be anything else to say. She looked up at me, smiled, and wafted off. I saw Dorcas looking my way. I put on my 'busy Sales Manager' look especially for her benefit, but it didn't fool Dorcas. She came up to me with two pre-lunch glasses of orange juice and handed me one. She said, 'She is most beautiful, yes?'

I said distantly, 'Who? Oh, Michelle Sherborne?' As though I was thinking of something else. 'Yes, I suppose so.'

'She is very interested in you, of course.'

'Me? Oh, nonsense, Dorcas.' But it is very difficult to offend a man by telling him that an attractive woman is interested in him, and I had trouble keeping the distant look.

Dorcas wasn't finished. 'You would not be human if you were not fluttered.'

'Flattered.'

'Thank you. Flattered. But there is one thing. Do you know how old Miss Sherborne is?'

I said, 'Really, Dorcas, this is – oh, nearly thirty, I suppose, if it matters.'

'She is twenty-one years old. You are thirty-six.' Dorcas looked at me. 'Before anything happens, you should perhaps ask yourself if you are intending to screw her – or adopt her?'

This deliberate crudity from Dorcas shocked me. It was as if a bishop had told a dirty joke. For a moment I felt a rush of anger and it was on the tip of my tongue to lash out at Dorcas for interfering in something which had nothing to do with her. Then I looked down at her face and saw on her delicate features a concern which I had never seen before. She smiled, as if to take away the sting of the words. Suddenly I saw the humour of it and laughed like hell. People were standing around before going into lunch and most of them looked my way. I said, 'Thank you, Dorcas,' and kissed her, which produced a brief round of ironic applause from my sales team. I put my arm around her and said, 'You are an interfering old busybody, but you are also a jewel.'

'Above all prices.'

'Price.'

'Thank you. Price. Now we go in for lunch.'

I wanted D-M to give the closing address but he refused. 'No, Tom. It is your conference and you should close it. I shall say a few words at dinner tonight, nothing prolonged, but this afternoon belongs to you.'

I'm no good at the pep-talk type of speech, the holy-roller, hot-gospeller sort of thing which is supposed to send the sales force out in a blaze of glory, ready to sell hailstorm insurance in the Sahara. Actually I don't believe in that sort of talk anyway. I believe that the danger is that you can insult the intelligence of the audience, and if there are any benefits from it, they are short-term at best. The next day the glow has faded and the salesman is back in the cut-and-thrust of his daily job and the talk is forgotten.

Anyway, I stood up and told the team that while nobody was pretending that their jobs were easy, from what they had seen and heard in the past three days it would be obvious that management was completely committed to doing everything possible to back them up. I said that I was at their service at all times if there was anything I could do to make their jobs easier. I ended up by saying that in the ten months I had held this job I had come to realise that I had a very fine team working with me, and I was proud of them.

It may not have been the greatest speech ever, but at least it was short and free of bullshit. I meant every word of it and that always seems to come across. Anyway, the boys were generous with their applause – but that could simply have been a sign of the relief they felt at not having to sit in the conference room a moment longer.

D-M stood up for just ten minutes at the banquet and thanked everyone for the work they had put in to make the conference a success, hoped they had enjoyed themselves, and said that the last evening was not for listening to speeches but for having fun. He could say that with no worries that anyone would dream of overdoing it; the Banquo's ghost of Jack Oxhill was present at every table in the room.

Sitting here in my room and going over the highlights of the conference, I realise that my estimation of D-M keeps rising. He is the archetype of a low-profile boss. He never throws his weight around, I have never heard him raise his voice, but he always seems to . . .

TEN MINUTES LATER. Well, well, well. That last paragraph didn't get finished, because there was a tap at my door and when I opened it Michelle walked in. She was wearing the same dress she had worn at the banquet, with a scoop neck that had my sales team's eyes popping out. Believe it or not, she was carrying a half-bottle of champagne and two glasses. She put them down, turned and stretched up to kiss me.

I nearly ruptured myself backing away from her. I was stunned; this sort of thing happens in 'Dallas' not to Tom Liskeard in an Irish conference centre. Michelle pouted. She said, 'Don't do that, Tom. You promised to thank me properly for my talk today; now's your chance.' Damn it, she moved in on me again.

She looked beautiful, she smelt beautiful, her breath on my face was warm and sweet, and I already knew from that time in my office what was waiting under that scoop neck. Just for one crazy moment I thought, what the hell, why not? Then Dorcas's words came to me. 'She is twenty-one. You are thirty-six.' I put my hands up. 'Michelle, I'm flattered that you are here, but I am a one-woman man and I just happen to be married to that woman.' As I said it, I realised how true the words were.

She said, 'And you are a long way from home, and you deserve to let your hair down for once. Don't be afraid, Tom; this is just between you and me.'

Then I found I was getting irritated. 'Michelle, get it into your head that it's not on. Even if I was single, fooling around with office colleagues is a mug's game. You say it's just between you and me?

161

Don't kid yourself. Somehow or other that sort of thing always gets out, and there goes my job in this company – and yours. You proved today that you are a real professional with a good future; don't chuck it away. Now off you go, and remember, this never happened.'

Suddenly she stopped acting like Irma la Douce and looked instead like a schoolgirl who has been ticked off by the Head. She went scarlet, her eyes filled with tears, and she mumbled, 'Sorry. I'm very sorry,' and left in a hurry.

So here I am after a mind-boggling scene. I wouldn't have believed it had happened, but there is the half-bottle of bubbly to prove that it wasn't a hallucination. I have suddenly had the idea that I deserve a glass of champagne. There, now I'm sipping it as I write this. I'm feeling very virtuous and also very relieved; I have the feeling that I have just escaped from the deepest trouble of my innocent young life.

Finish the bottle, Liskeard, and go to bed, hoping that your recording angel is awake at this hour and busily getting it all down.

September

3 Monday

I was hardly back in the office last week when Jimmy Liss, the Chief Order Clerk, walked in waving a sheet of paper with a large grin all over his face. 'Like to see what happened to the sales figures while the whole lot of you were drinking Scotch?' He plonked the sheet down in front of me. 'Twenty-two per cent higher than the same period last month. Moral of this story? Get rid of the entire sales force, fire the whole bunch of them, and sales will go through the roof.'

I laughed. I like Jimmy, and his order clerks do a good job in not always ideal conditions. Customers tend to blame the person on the other end of the phone for stock shortages, delayed deliveries and dirty letters from the credit department, none of which are the order clerk's fault.

What is it that causes the sales in a territory to rise the moment you take the sales person out of that territory for a few days? I used to get frustrated – and worried, too – when I was away on a course and came back to find that my customers had seemed to wait for me to leave before writing or phoning in some terrific orders. You can only hope that your boss realises that it was you who initiated the orders, no matter when they came in, but it's a weird thing, all the same.

I made a decision and told Dorcas about the late-night visitor to my hotel room. She nodded. 'I thought she might do that. Of course, you sent her bagging?'

'Packing.'

'Thank you. Packing.'

I said, 'Yes, Dorcas, I did, but there was a moment when . . .' I looked at her. 'How did you know I would turn her down?'

Dorcas fluttered her delicate hands. 'Is like a scale, yes? You balance what you can get with what you can lose. Then is no contest.'

163

I thought of what I had to lose: not my job, but the three people I went home to every night. 'Right. There's no contest.' I had a last thought. 'Do you think I ought to tell Annabel?'

Dorcas sighed. 'Tom, have you lost your mind? You think Annabel will say, "That's my good, faithful husband"? Annabel is a wonderful person, but she is a woman, and I am telling you that she would never forgive you because another woman tried to get you into bed.'

'But I threw her out! I came out of that as pure as Saint Anna!'

'Doesn't matter.'

Oh.

October

2 Tuesday

Back from a wonderful holiday in Cornwall, hence the gap in the diary. Took my leave earlier this year to fit in with Annabel's brother and his family; their children and ours get along fine which makes it easier for the adults to have fun. Back to the usual slim sheaf of papers from Dorcas and a morning of dictating letters, phoning back people who had called and clearing up the few things that Dorcas and Dickie hadn't been able to handle.

I left the salesmen's individual sales figures until last, yelled for coffee, put my feet up and went through the printout sheets one by one. I already knew that the overall figures were on target; the first thing a new father asks when he gets home at night is, 'How's the baby?' The first thing a Sales Manager asks when he gets back to the office after a time away is, 'How are the figures?'

The first disappointment was Ken Milburn. All the way across the product range his sales were below target. I cursed. What to do – haul him in and ask him if his domestic life was going through another crisis? I vetoed that. I had done more to help him through his problems than most managers would have done, and I was not about to walk that road with him again. Go out into his territory with him and see if I could get him going again? No. I made a note to talk to D-M about getting rid of Ken. I had the authority to hire and fire without having to go upstairs but I felt that D-M would like to know that I was taking such a drastic step.

Then I put a line through the note. The time has come for me to do this sort of thing without running to papa. I made a new note – to call Ken in and give him my decision.

I flipped through more printout sheets and generally liked what I was seeing. I made a few notes to talk to individual salesmen about this and that, but on the whole things were going pretty well.

Then I hit the sheet for Brian Hook. Damn! Brian had been in his territory for five months now and his performance was not far short of hopeless. What was wrong? He seemed to be the ideal person for the job; I had thought so, the recruiting agency had thought so, even D-M had nodded approvingly when I had asked him his opinion. We had put him through the standard product training course and his marks had been well above average. I had spent time with him in the field, I had sent him out with some of my best men; he had received, if anything, more training and supervision than most. I made a note to get him in for a straight talk and this meant bringing him out of his territory overnight, but it had to be done. I had an unhappy feeling that the talk wasn't going to do any good, and that he was destined to go the same route that Ken Milburn was headed for – out.

The thing is, I hate the idea of dismissing someone after six months; it looks so bad on their CV the next time they look for a job. I reminded myself that I was running a sales division not a boy scout camp.

Dorcas stuck her head in. 'Mr Oxhill to see you.' I nodded. I hadn't seen Jack since Ireland, and I wondered what sort of tone I should adopt with him. Brisk, neutral and, of course, no mention of his *débâcle* at the conference. He walked in, sat down and grinned at me. 'Hullo, Tom. I don't have to waste your time this morning; I came in to say that I've been offered another job and I'm accepting it.'

One to D-M, I thought; he foresaw this. I said, 'All right, Jack. I hope that it's the right move for you and that you will be happy in it.'

He said, 'Well, it's such a good offer that I can't refuse it, much as I hate to leave Hutton Horner.'

I thought, now that's a fair amount of chutzpah, chum, considering what went on at our last meeting. He was talking as though he still had a bright future with HH. Anyway, least said soonest repaired, as Dorcas once said, and I didn't feel that there was any mileage to be gained by reminding him why he had left the conference early. He said, and for the first time he wasn't quite so cocky. 'Er . . . can I hope for a decent reference from you, Tom? For old times' sake?'

Mentally I thanked D-M for his strict policy on this. 'Jack, Hutton Horner doesn't give references. All I'm allowed to give you is a letter stating your dates of joining and leaving, your position in the company, and your salary at the time you left.'

He looked disappointed. 'Oh. Yes, well, that's that, then. I would

166

like to leave at the end of the month, if that's not too much of a hassle for you. These people want me to start as soon as possible.'

If he was waiting for me to ask him who 'these people' were, then he was going to wait some time. He rose and stuck his hand out. 'Well, I suppose that there's nothing more to say, except that I'd like to say . . .' He seemed about to make a speech, but I had had as much of Jack Oxhill as I could take for one day and I hustled him out. I phoned D-M and told him that his prediction had come true. 'If his new employer telephones you and asks about him, what do you propose to say?'

My God! I hadn't thought of that. 'Hell, D-M, what can I say? He's not a bad salesman, you know. Have I the right to wreck his prospects because of one sidestep?'

'Tom, you can't hide what happened. If you were on the other side, you would expect the truth from his former employer. By all means, stress his good points – his field performance and so on. Give him a chance, at least.' I put the phone down hoping that Jack's new boss wouldn't phone.

Back to the salesmen's printouts and there was good news from a sales*person*. Wendy Carlton was really doing well. Not only were her sales figures good; she was also opening new accounts and keeping a tight rein on her slow payers. Six months ago I had hired two sales people; now one of them seemed to be turning out a hopeless case and the other was a star. Not good enough; no manager looks good with a fifty per cent strike rate on hiring staff.

Later, at home, I received a telephone call. 'Tom! Good to hear your voice. Hubert here.' For a moment I wondered who Hubert was, then I remembered the recruitment people, the head-hunters. What he wanted to know was whether I was at all interested in meeting the top management of the company who needed a Sales Manager.

I said, 'You mean to say they are still looking? It's been eight months since you first spoke to me.'

Hubert coughed. 'Well, Tom, the truth is that they did take a man, but he has proved to be', he coughed again, 'not really suitable.'

I thought, yes, I can relate to that problem. Then it struck me that I was talking to the crowd who had lumbered me with Brian Hook, but I didn't say so. *Then* I realised that Hubert's nervous cough probably meant that the man who had proved to be not really suitable for the Sales Manager's job had also been recommended by Hubert and his merry men, but I choked back a comment on that thought as well. I said, 'I really don't think it would be worth while. I'm getting the hang of this job and I'm happy where I am.'

Hubert said, 'Well, I respect your decision on that, but I must tell you that we are not going to give up on you.' This didn't sound as though he was respecting my decision, but we parted without any feathers being ruffled.

I put down the phone and said to Annabel, 'Hard to be humble when you're perfect in every way.'

Without bothering to raise her head from her sewing she said, 'Your little headhunters again? They don't give up, do they? Why do they keep phoning *you*, though? Surely there are plenty of good Sales Managers?'

'Plenty of good ones, but not many of us fantastic ones.' She threw a cushion at me.

I don't want to change my company; I'm fairly sure of that. I like what I do and where I do it. What I *have* realised over this past year, though, is that I like working for Harold Dunsby-Martin. I can see now that one of the most important aspects of a job, perhaps the most important, is: *who is directly above you.* I never understood this before, and it puts a heavy responsibility on me. I am to a large extent the most important single thing about the job of twenty-three people. Some of them are certainly where they are because I am where I am. Take Dan Lathom, for instance, who was a wash-out under Bert and is very competent under me. That sounds conceited, but it isn't; who knows, with another manager Brian Hook could take off like a rocket.

MEMO TO ME: Take great care, Liskeard, in everything you say and do. To a certain degree, you affect the destinies of twenty-three people.

October

10 Wednesday

Two important interviews today, both educational, if I have the
sense to learn from them.

First, Ken Milburn. I had called him in for a very straight talk,
with the possibility that the talk would end with my dismissing him.
He walked in and sat down and there was something different about
him; he looked somehow as though he was in charge of himself. He
said, 'Tom, I know why you have got me in today.'

I said, 'You do?'

'Yes. It's about my rotten showing over the past few months. Let
me save you some time. You have been more than patient with me
and I'm grateful for the trouble you have taken, and for very little
return on my part. I wouldn't be surprised if you were considering
firing me.' I opened my mouth to speak but he had the bit in his
teeth. 'Tom, three days ago Joanne and I had it out once and for all
and we have decided to separate. I'm saying nothing against her, but
we are simply not meant for each other. Joanne has a very strong
personality and without meaning to, she has been smothering me.'
He squared his shoulders. 'Give me two months, Tom, and I
promise I will show you what I can do. I feel a new man already, and I
am going to make you proud of me.' He grabbed my hand and
pumped away at it. I said something, I don't remember what, but it
must have been what he wanted to hear. He marched out of the office
as though he was ready to take on the entire Albanian army.

Dorcas put her head round the door. 'I am betting that he has got
rid of his wife.'

'Or she has got rid of him.'

She shook her head. '*Il est peu probable*. That sort of woman tries
to hold on to her possessions. No matter; now he will be a man.'

I read in Bert Corley's book that it is a good idea to interview the

169

spouse of an applicant for a job as well as the applicant, and I remember thinking, cowcake; you hire the person, not the family. Now I wonder. All right, Ken Milburn; you have your two months, and let's all keep our fingers crossed for you.

The second interview was very different. Brian Hook came in this afternoon, as arranged, and slouched in a chair. He said, 'What's up, Doc?' in an imitation of Bugs Bunny.

I stared at him. 'What's up? Brian, is it possible that you don't know why you are here?'

'Haven't a clue, Tom. Oh, if it's about that dent in the car door, I explained about that in my report. This other fellow – '

'It is not about a dent in your car.' I waved his printout at him. 'Brian, when you get a copy of this every month, doesn't it occur to you that the row of minus figures in the right-hand column is a clear indication that you are hopelessly short of target all through the range?'

He looked surprised. 'Am I? Oh, I didn't realise it was as bad as all that.'

'You didn't *realise?*' I was speechless. I tried again. 'But the printout tells you the whole story.'

Brian smiled crookedly and scratched his head. 'Well, to tell you the truth, Tom, I never pay much attention to those things, those – what do you call them – printouts. All those figures, you know.'

'All – those – figures.' I stood up and sat down. The one thing I wanted to do more than anything else in the world just then was to kill him. I took some slow, deep breaths which didn't help. As quietly and calmly as I could, I said, 'You spent two days in your training period on paperwork. You were taught that the most important piece of paper a salesman ever handles is the computer printout relating to his territory because it gives him a complete picture of everything which is going on in that territory. And you tell me that you don't even *read* it? Tell me – do you even take it out of the envelope?'

He shrugged his shoulders. 'Well, you know – '

I said, 'Do you realise that you have left me no choice but to fire you? Do you understand that, in a way, you have just fired yourself?'

I don't know what reaction I had expected, but Brian frowned and nodded slowly, exactly as though he and I had been discussing an interesting debating point and had come to the same conclusion about it. He said, 'Yes, that's probably the best thing.'

'Damn it, Brian, I hate to do this.' I found an almost apologetic

170

tone creeping into my voice and pushed it out. Brian had no apology coming from me. 'You came across so well when I first interviewed you. You chaired your session at the sales conference better than anyone else. The report on you from the recruiting agency was first-rate.' I shook my head. 'I think that this was partly my fault; I should have stayed closer to you in the beginning.'

'Oh, no, Tom; you did all you could and I'm grateful for the time you spent with me. Sorry it didn't work out better.'

I said, 'Look, officially I'm not going to dismiss you because it won't look well on your track record. Find another job in the next couple of months and resign, and you can say – oh, that you wanted a change, or something like that.'

Brian smiled and shook his head. 'Tom, you are a nice person. Thanks, but that won't be necessary. I think I'll just take some time off from work, perhaps go to Australia for a while. There's a girl I know who lives in Melbourne and she has been phoning, asking me to come and stay.'

I goggled at him. 'You mean, just give up working? But what will you live on?'

He wrinkled his nose and looked a bit embarrassed.'Well, as it happens I'm lucky in that respect. My Dad died three years ago and left me pretty well provided for. Trouble is, it can get a bit boring sometimes, not having a job.'

Saints and angels. That was it. That was the missing piece in the jigsaw puzzle called Brian Hook. Intelligent, engaging, articulate and presentable; everything going for him except one little thing – *he didn't have to work.*

Brian was standing with his hand out. 'Sorry it didn't work out, Tom. Waste of time and effort for you, I'm afraid.' He smiled. 'No hard feelings?'

I shook his hand. 'No hard feelings, Brian. Have a good time in Australia.'

I had to tell D-M about this, and a call on the intercom wouldn't do; I wanted to see his face. Evelyn waved me through to his office and as I walked in through the door I blurted out, 'I've just fired Brian Hook.'

He nodded slowly. 'A lost cause, I'm afraid. Yet he seemed a sure bet. I wonder what – '

I interrupted. 'D-M, it appears that he has a private income inherited from his father. He is independently wealthy.'

D-M's head jerked up. 'Good God! Of course. No need to work,

171

no motivation, no – *pressure* of any sort. I imagine he works because he gets bored with not working.'

I nodded. 'He said so, in so many words.'

'Yes. Shakespeare said it, you know, "If all the year were playing holidays, To sport would be as tedious as to work." But the routine of work quickly bored him even more, I suppose.' D-M slapped his desk, something I have never seen him do. 'Do you know, that is the one question I have never thought to ask job applicants.'

I said, 'But damn it, D-M, you can't say to someone "How well off are you? Do you really have to work?"'

He said, 'Can't you?'

We stared at each other.

172

October

15 Monday

One of the letters which had been waiting for me when I returned from leave was from Tweedledum and Tweedledee, the sales training twins. Had I thought further about engaging training consultants, it asked, to give my sales people the ammunition which they so urgently needed in the battlefield of today's competitive markets, and could they assist me in my decision in any way?

I phoned Evelyn Street and asked for some of D-M's time. It is all very well for D-M to tell me that his door is always open; what he neglects to say is that outside that door sits Evelyn, and sometimes it seems that she believes her job is to keep her boss totally submerged in a sterile saline solution, out of reach of possible infection from people like me. We have had one or two fairly sharp words, but we are going through a period of *détente* at the moment. She told me to come right up, that Mr Dunsby-Martin was free for ten minutes. I said, 'Evelyn, I need a lot more than that. Say an hour.'

'Oh.' I actually heard her suck in her breath. I felt like saying, 'I haven't made an indecent suggestion, you silly old ratbag. I merely want to see my immediate superior regarding a matter of importance to the welfare and prosperity of the organisation which pays your inflated salary.' I didn't say it, of course; I make up speeches like that and they sound fine while I'm shaving but I never actually say them out loud. Eventually Evelyn admitted reluctantly that she could probably squeeze me in at four this afternoon.

I took all the Proselling bumf up as well as some figures of my own and announced to D-M that the time had come to do something permanent about sales training. He said, 'Have you decided which is better, an outside firm or our own man?' He always manages to pre-empt me.

I showed him the stuff from the trainers as well as my own figures,

173

and went over my list of the advantages of having an in-company trainer.

D-M said, 'You like the idea of having a Hutton Horner man, rather than these outside people?' I said yes, for the reasons I'd given. 'Very well, Tom. Any idea of where to get him?'

'I could get hold of those recruiting people we used before.' I had a tiny shock when I realised that I had nearly called them 'head-hunters', which could have let the cat out of the bag. 'Or newspaper advertising, of course.'

'You might get hold of our advertising agency. Ask their Media Manager – Evelyn has his name – if there exists a trade magazine aimed at training. Probably the best place to advertise.' Why didn't I think of that.

Then D-M said something else I hadn't thought of. 'Is it possible that the man we want could already be in the company?' I said that it was possible, of course; I hadn't thought about it. 'Circulate a copy of the advertisement when you have drawn it up. You never know, we might have a potential trainer in our midst. And Tom,' he said as I was leaving, 'don't forget to say in the advertisement that our staff are aware of the vacancy.' I looked blank. He said, 'Suppose you were interested in a job being advertised but no company's name appeared on the advertisement, is it not possible that you could hesitate to apply for it in case the company turned out to be your own.'

And what a good thought. You learn something new every day, Liskeard, so long as your mind, like D-M's door, is always open.

October

19 Friday

A confrontation with one of my people. Damn it, I'm getting too old for this sort of thing.

After my talk with D-M I got an advertisement together and we put it into the evening papers and in one of the training journals. I suggested morning papers as well, but Cyril Headley of Personnel said no. 'You don't want someone who has time to read a morning paper when they should be working.' Typical outlook of a personnel person, but a point, I suppose.

I also stuck a copy on the bulletin board and sent copies to all the sales people, and that was what caused this morning's fracas. Dorcas appeared and said, 'Mr Bishop to see you.'

'Guy? What's he want?' Stupid question.

'I do not know. He is looking triumphal.'

'Triumphant.'

'Thank you. Triumphant.'

'Good. Show him in.' If one of my top salesmen was looking triumphant it meant that he had netted an enormous order, and I can always stand that sort of news. For Guy to leave his territory in the middle of a working day was most unusual, and he had probably come to do a spot of bragging. Fine!

Guy strode in and yes, he did look triumphant. He threw himself into a chair and tossed a sheet of paper across the desk. He said, 'Look no further, Tom. I'm your man.'

Only then did I see that the piece of paper was not a signed order for six figures; it was a copy of the advertisement for a sales trainer. I looked at Guy and knew that here was a problem. I said, 'You, Guy? You want to be a sales trainer? What on earth for?'

'What for? What sort of question is that? Because it would be a step up, of course. I don't intend to be a salesman all my life, that's why. Come on, Tom. You know I'm the best qualified of all the boys for this job. My track record shows it.'

I wondered how best to handle this. I knew that with someone like Guy Bishop I couldn't pussyfoot around it, I would have to give it to him naked and unadorned. I said, 'Guy, you are one of my best salesmen – perhaps even the best, if sales volume is the only criterion – but you are not the man for this job.'

His face was hard. 'No? Give me one reason why not, and it had better be a bloody good one.'

I said, 'I'll give you three. One, you sell as though the hounds of hell were behind you – but, Guy, you don't sell according to the book. You break all the rules and you get away with breaking the rules because you are a natural-born salesman. Now, that's wonderful and I wish I had ten more like you, but that's not what I need in a sales trainer. He will *have* to operate within the rules.' Guy sat there with his eyes fixed on my face. 'Two, a trainer in this company would not only be doing sales training; he would cover *all* training, and that includes taking new sales people through such things as the administration of a sales territory. Guy, your slow payers are always over the maximum, your returns are always late, and your territory coverage is at best, questionable.' I took a breath. 'Three – and don't think I'm enjoying this – when you gave that talk on prospecting at the sales conference you talked *down* to your audience. Your attitude was, "If you were as good as me, this is the way you would do it". Now that sort of tone is the kiss of death for anyone who has to stand up and talk in public – and standing up and talking is what a trainer does.'

It was just as though I hadn't spoken. Guy put his fists on the desk and said, 'Tom, I want that job. I deserve it and it's mine!' There was a lot that I could have said but it occurred to me that I had already said it, so I replied, 'No.'

He stood up so abruptly that his chair fell over. 'I'm not accepting this. I'm taking it higher.'

I said, 'Guy, please don't do that.' As I said the words I realised that it sounded as though I was begging him on my account, and something in his expression showed that he had taken it that way. He turned and left.

Dorcas came in and saw me putting the chair back on its feet. 'Mr Bishop is agitated?'

'Mr Bishop is agitated. Mr Bishop is at this moment on his way to an interview which will ruin his prospects in this company.'

Dorcas pursed her lips. 'Ah. He did not get whatever it was he wanted from you, so now he goes to Mr Dunsby-Martin. What foolishness.' I showed her the copy of the advertisement which Guy had brought in. 'Mr Bishop wants to be a trainer? Never in this world. He is – *pas le type.*'

'My thoughts exactly.' I thought of phoning D-M to warn him that Guy was on his way to his own destruction but I didn't. Firstly, Guy could very well have had second thoughts about bearding the boss in his den and if so, why drag D-M in? Least said, soonest repaired. Secondly, I didn't think that D-M needed any warning about anything whatever, even the coming of the Second Flood.

Guy hadn't had any second thoughts. D-M phoned through half an hour later. He said with no preamble, 'Pity about Bishop.'

For a moment I wondered if he meant that I had made the wrong decision about Guy.

I said, 'You don't think he's the man for the job, do you?'

'What, Bishop? For sales trainer? Last man, very last. Leonard would do a better job; really would.' Leonard is D-M's driver. He went on, 'I told him that it was your decision in any event, but that if it made any difference, I agreed with you. I also said that as far as I was concerned, his visit to my office had never taken place.' He paused. 'Not true, of course; one can never expunge the incident from one's memory. Still, one has to say something like that. Hope we can keep him – one of your best men, is he not?'

'He is, and I very much want to keep him, but for the moment the ball is in his court. He'll resign or he won't, and there isn't much I can do.'

'Of course not. It seems that you handled it well.'

Perhaps, perhaps not. Well, I am going to have to start hiring sales people again; two to replace Brian Hook and Jack Oxhill, and maybe three if Guy does leave. Also, I shall need another one to train up so that he can eventually take over half of David Lundy's territory; the potential in Wales is getting to be too much for one man to handle.

A sales trainer and extra sales people; Cyril Headley is going to cry like a baby about my staff budget.

177

November

5 Monday

Long time since I have had the time or energy to write up the diary and my family has seen damn little of me over the past four weeks. Hutton Horner has always had a policy of manufacturing up to a standard, not down to a price, which means that we tend to be slightly on the high side price-wise compared with our competitors.

Now, this is fine and, generally speaking, our customers buy from us because they know that they get that little bit more for the few pounds extra that the product costs – touch of class, so to speak.

Except when disaster strikes, as it did about a month ago. The Chief Quality Controller in the factory was a rehabilitated alcoholic and Mac McLeod had taken him on only because he was an excellent man and because he was regularly attending therapy meetings.

Well, he had had a sudden domestic upheaval and it had been enough to push him over the edge again. This was, of course, a personal tragedy for him, but it was also a disaster for the company. A complete run of swing-bin liners was produced – tonnes of them – with insufficient heat-sealing. This would normally have been picked up immediately the run had started, but the QC man had let the run proceed right through to its end. So ten thousand housewives found that when they lifted the liners out of their bins their potato peelings, wet tea-bags and other unmentionables fell on to the kitchen floor.

What do you do in a situation where the fault is absolutely and entirely yours? You pull out all the stops, that's what you do. If you are the Production Engineer you more or less give up any idea of luxuries like sleep, because part of your factory is on three shifts, twenty-four hours a day. If you are the Managing Director you make a few tough policy decisions like two-for-one: the customer brings one packet of liners back and gets two in exchange. If you are the Sales Manager you pack a bag, kiss your wife goodbye and visit

178

customer after customer, telling the same story over and over again. Most of my sales people could have handled the problem by themselves but I felt, and D-M backed me up, that when the company lets its good customers down it is up to management to get out there and eat some humble pie along with the sales people. I forgot to say that D-M himself made some calls on some of our biggest customers.

The whole exercise has cost HH a king's ransom, but we have come out at the other end of it with our quality image restored. In fact, in a weird way the whole thing might have done us some good. As soon as our customers saw that we were going to make good every penny, and a lot more, they mucked in and co-operated very well. As one East Anglian wholesaler said, 'So Hutton Horner made a mistake? Only proves you're human, mate.' Many people seemed to feel complimented that the National Sales Manager had taken the trouble to come all the way from London to give them the assurances that they needed – I had my hand shaken warmly many times. Even now, our old customers are still very much on our side.

Dorcas had an explanation for this. 'What are you thinking of the service we get from the word-processor people?'

I said, 'Terrific. They are right on the ball. Real professionals.'

'Yes, but do you remember when I first got it? The troubles?'

'Oh, Lord, yes; everything went wrong that could go wrong.' I remembered. £3,500 worth of word-processor and nothing but hassles, but the service department of the company commanded my admiration with the way they tackled the problems. Nothing was too much trouble, they freely admitted that the fault was theirs, not ours, and eventually they got it going properly. They sent Dorcas flowers for being so patient, too; a nice gesture, I thought.

Dorcas said, 'So. When nothing goes wrong, people say, "Oh, yes, is quite a good company." But when something goes wrong and they fix it brilliantly, people say, "What a grand company that one is!"'

She's right, of course. I tremble to think what we would look like now if we had been just a tiny bit grudging in admitting fault, or had been reluctant about replacing the goods, or if we had not gone out into the field in sackcloth and ashes.

MEMO TO ME: When the fault is yours, admit it freely and at once. Try to hide and the wolf-pack is on you; come out into the open and you could end up looking like Saint Bernard.

All the same, I don't want to go through it again for a while, thank you.

November

14 Wednesday

Oh, hell and damnation. I think I may have made a very big mistake, and it is a people mistake, which is always worse than a thing mistake. Sitting here, I am looking back at it and wondering if there was anything else I could have done.

What happened was a telephone call from a customer, Julius Venn. I know him well, because when I carried an order book he was in my territory. It is a big company and Julius himself is a very straight character; we had a good customer/salesman relationship. No, come to think of it, it was more than that. We came to be friends.

I said, 'Julius! What can I do for you today?'

He said, 'Hello, Tom. Jack Oxhill.'

'Oxhill? Yes, he was in my team.'

'I know. He applied for a job here and I have taken him on, subject to his getting a good reference from you.' I had the feeling that I was not about to enjoy this conversation. 'Now he has brought in this chit from you, but it gives me nothing about him, the man himself, how he did his job, or anything like that.'

'That's all we are allowed to put on paper, Julius; company policy.'

'I know; good old company policy.' He sounded cynical. 'Never mind what you can put on paper, Tom. What about just the two of us on the telephone? He tells me that he left Hutton Horner because of a difference of opinion between the two of you. What about it?'

Damn Jack Oxhill for putting me on this spot. I took a quick decision. 'Julius, first of all let me say this. Jack is a very good salesman. He was always on target, he got on well with the customers, and he wasn't afraid of hard work. Not a clock-watcher.'

'So? What are you holding back, Tom?'

180

Oh, shit. 'Well, it wasn't a difference of opinion. What happened was that at our sales conference in Ireland he had a few drinks too many and made a fool of himself. Now, Julius, that was one stupid mistake in three years of good work. He has certainly learnt his lesson and I'm sure he won't do it again.'

There was a silence at the other end, then I heard Julius sigh. 'Thank you, Tom. I have decided not to employ Mr Oxhill.'

In a panic I said, 'Julius! For getting a little tight one night with his friends?'

'No, Tom. To get drunk at a convention is nothing. What he did wrong was to lie to me. If he had told me the truth, I would have taken him without a second thought, but I cannot afford to have someone in my employ who will lie to me. Thank you, Tom. My respects to Mrs Liskeard. Shalom.'

He hung up, leaving me with a piece of dead plastic pressed against my ear and my heart in my boots.

I didn't bother to tell D-M because I knew exactly what he would say. 'Nothing else you could do. Unfortunate, but there it is. Don't concern yourself about it; Oxhill brought it on himself, I'm afraid.' All very well, but Jack Oxhill has a nice wife and three small children, and I have just done him out of a job.

Good day's work, Liskeard. Now that you are home, why not beat your wife, curse the brats and kick the cat?

November

16 Friday

The letters are beginning to come in about the sales training job, and I look through them before passing them on to Cyril Headley for preliminary vetting. Cyril doesn't know anything about sales training, of course, but he does know the parameters (lord, now I'm beginning to use that horrible word) within which our man must stand, and he can throw out the non-doers and the no-hopers without my having to waste time on them. Of the first four letters, two are from salesmen with no experience of training, and two are from trainers with no experience of selling. Marvellous!

I'm writing this just after 6.30. Annabel's birthday was yesterday and mine is tomorrow, so of course we always go out to dinner on November 16. I'm looking forward to fooling around with the CD player we bought as a combination present, together with some discs – Verdi and Tchaikovsky for her, Waylon Jennings and Willie Nelson for me. The sitter has just turned up and Annabel has come out of the bathroom looking like a teenager instead of a mother of two. She has asked me if I can stop scribbling long enough to take a middle-aged, toil-worn old drudge out to dinner.

Whoopee!

November

22 Thursday

This time, in my advertisement for salespeople, I am making the point that women are welcome to apply. Last time I advertised I did say 'salespeople' and not 'salesmen,' but I wasn't really looking for females. Wendy Carlton is doing such a tremendous job out there, though, that I would dearly love a couple more like her to replace Hook and Oxhill.

Interesting thought. Now that I have overcome my suspicion of and, all right, prejudice against women in the sales force, what if we had an application for the Sales Trainer job from a woman who had all the qualifications and experience we need; would I take her on? I know that earlier this year I would have said, 'No dice,' but now, do you know, I believe I would. If she was tough enough to handle my bunch of delinquents, it might be the best thing in the world for them to be trained by a woman.

I'll mention it to Cyril Headley tomorrow and spoil the day for that bigoted, chauvinistic old grump.

December

3 Monday

Well, I'm still trying to believe it. I am sitting here with a glass of bubbly, Annabel is on the phone to her mother giving her the news, and even Pete and Angie are excited, although they are not quite certain what it's all about.

It started this morning with a call from Evelyn Street that I was to present myself at her office at 12.15 precisely. I didn't know what D-M wanted me for, but what was unusual was Evelyn saying, 'And Mr Dunsby-Martin says that you should put your jacket on.'

I remembered that someone had mentioned that there was to be a Board meeting this morning, so the jacket warning meant that I was going to have to present myself in the holy of holies. D-M never minds if I come to his office in my shirt sleeves, although he never takes his own jacket off in the office. My attendance in the boardroom usually means good news rather than bad; D-M wanting the Directors to get some dope about the Sales Division from me personally, rather than second-hand from him. I appreciate this; it is always nice to bring good news to the bosses.

As I proceeded upstairs in good time, Dorcas having checked the knot in my tie and frowned at my hair, I thought that what the Board probably wanted to hear from me was a run-down on the quality control disaster and the way we had managed it, and I was happy that the Sales Division in general and Tom Liskeard in particular had come out of it with no blood shed and just a few bruises as a reminder of the episode.

Evelyn smiled at me and looked as though she was on the point of saying something, but she ushered me into the boardroom without a word. As I walked in, the Directors all stood up. I stopped; this was something new. They were all smiling at me, and D-M came round from his place at the top of the table and shook my hand. He said,

184

'Tom, I won't make a speech. I shall merely tell you that this morning the Board unanimously voted to create a new place at this table. From February next year you will be the Sales Director of Hutton Horner. Congratulations!'

All the Directors applauded and each one came and shook my hand. Then they sat down and looked at me. They obviously expected me to say something but my brain was whirling around up there with the stars and planets. I said, 'Gentlemen, I am speechless, which is an unusual position for a salesman to be in. All I can say is that I have just had the most exciting news of my business life, and I will do everything in my power to make sure that you won't regret your decision.' It must have been all right because they clapped again, and then Evelyn came in and handed round sherry from a tray.

After the sherry they all shook my hand again, which was a nice way of saying, 'go away now because you won't be sitting at this table until February and right now we have business to discuss.' I found my way back to my office in a daze. Dorcas said, 'You are back soon after talking to those important people?'

I said, 'Uh-huh,' or words to that effect.

She peered at me and said, 'You smell of drink. In the middle of the day? *Du liebe!*' Her eyes opened wide. 'You have been having drink with the Directors; *alors*, you are yourself a Director, yes?' I nodded. She screamed and put her arms around me. 'I knew it! I knew it!'

'Take it easy, woman, you are throttling me. And you didn't know it; you couldn't.'

'Oh, yes, I did know. Not today, no, but I knew you would be a Director in God's time.'

'Oh? Why?' I asked.

She stopped smiling. 'Because you are good in your job. I have worked for many managers in many countries. You are perhaps the best.' She looked at me and I saw that her eyes were full of tears. She kissed me and hugged me again and turned away very quickly and grabbed for tissues from her desk. Then of course *I* had to start getting all choked up and emotional. I said, 'Dorcas, I love you.'

She made a Hungarian noise and said, 'I make coffee.'

Annabel has told me to get that stupid book out of my lap because she intends to sit in it, which sounds very sexy until Pete and Angie climb up, too, and demand to be allowed to taste the fizzy drink.

What a day.

December

19 Wednesday

I see that the last entry in the diary ended with the comment 'What a day!' It is nearly a year since I started writing in this book, and as Huckleberry Finn said, 'If I'd known what a pain in the arse it was going to be, I'd never have done it,' or words to that effect. This will be the last entry; I'm running out of pages anyway, and I've done what I set out to do, which was to put down the highs and lows, glories and catastrophies of my day-to-day job for one year.

Also it is getting to be the time for office parties and social parties and buying Christmas presents, and I am touching the ground in spots. I'll put the diary away and pull it out in five years' time and see what a chump I made of myself way back when.

Two things happened today and I'll put them down, because they represent a sort of low and a high in my year.

The first thing was a telephone call from Jack Oxhill. His voice was hard and biting as he said, 'I just phoned to wish you a merry Christmas, Tom, and to ask you if you feel pleased with yourself. It's not enough that you throw me out of my job, you also make damned sure that I don't get another one. What sort of Christmas do you think my family will have this year?'

I thought to myself, 'Oh, my God.' To Jack I said, 'Jack, that's not fair. One, I did not throw you out, you resigned. I could have fired you, but I let you resign in your own time. Two, when Mr Venn phoned me and told me the story you gave him about personality differences between you and me, and asked me if it was true, what else could I have said? Do you think that he wouldn't have found out the truth? And he did not turn you down because you got smashed at the conference – he did it because you lied to him. If you had told him the truth you would have been working for him now, so don't blame me.'

There was silence at the other end. Then I heard the receiver being replaced. Only then did I realise what a bloody fool I had been. At least before the call he had had the small satisfaction of being able to blame me for his problems; now I had carefully pointed out that it was all his own fault.

Nice work, Liskeard. Merry Christmas.

Sales managers are supposed to keep a bottle of vodka in their desk drawers, just like private eyes on TV. I swear that if I'd had a bottle just then I would have thrown back three fingers of it.

Dorcas put her head around the door. 'Mr Bishop.'

Wonderful. All I needed was another session with Guy Bishop, who would probably tell me that I had buggered up *his* life, too. I said wearily, 'Does he look triumphal?'

Dorcas said, 'Triumphant.'

'Thank you. Triumphant?'

'No.'

'All right. Herd him in.'

Guy walked in and sat down. He looked at me and shook his head. 'Tom, the last time I was in this room I made a fool of myself.'

I said, 'This room is used to that. I do it here about once a week.'

'Not the size I made of myself. Tom, you were right. What the hell made me think I wanted to be a trainer, for God's sake? To stand up in front of a group and say, "Now, fellows, this is the product and that is the customer, and we are going to spend the next week in this bloody room trying to get them together".' He laughed. 'That's not me. I am a first-class salesman, right?'

I said, 'Right. One of the very best.'

'When I left your office I went crying to Dunsby-Martin, and of course he sent me off with a whole colony of fleas in my ear. He was good enough to say that as far as he was concerned the conversation hadn't taken place.' Guy made a face. 'Well, maybe he means it, maybe not. Anyway, I don't want *you* to forget my stupidity, Tom; in fact, I want you to remind me of it every now and then. I am a *salesman*. Don't ever let me forget that.'

I said, 'Welcome back, Guy. There aren't many as good as you, and I don't want to lose you.'

He looked at his watch. 'Do you realise that we have been on unpaid overtime for seven minutes? How about a quick snort? I'm buying.'

I said, 'When I say that it's the best offer I've had all day long, you won't believe how true it is.'

As I said, the previous entry in the diary ended with the comment, 'What a day!' I could end this entry by saying, what a year. When I got home, I told Annabel about the two interviews – one very minus, one very plus. She kissed me and went to the bookshelves and came back with a book of quotations open at something that Samuel Butler wrote.

Life is like playing a violin in public, and learning the instrument as one goes along.

Now they tell me.